Halloween Coloring Book

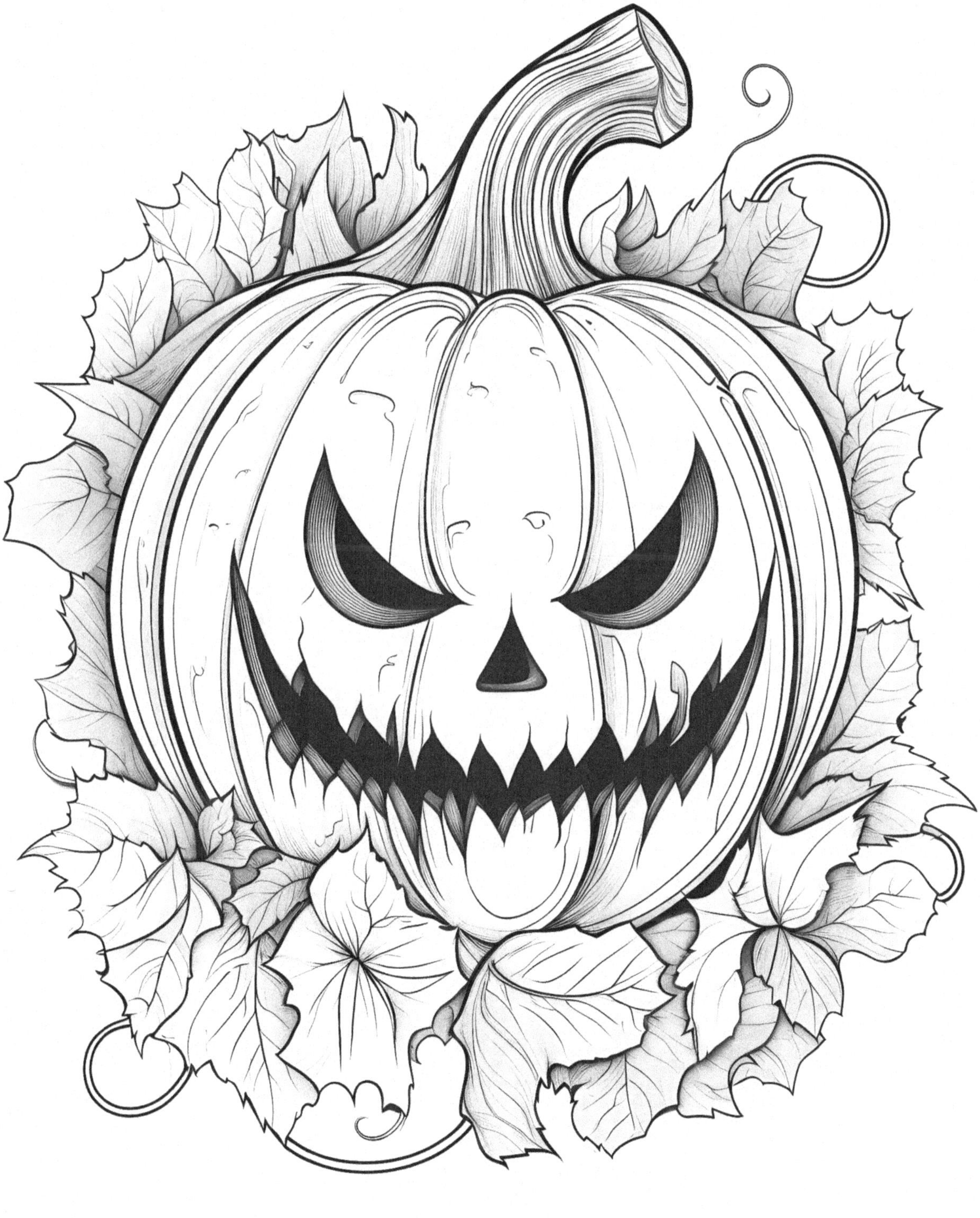

THIS BOOK BELONGS TO

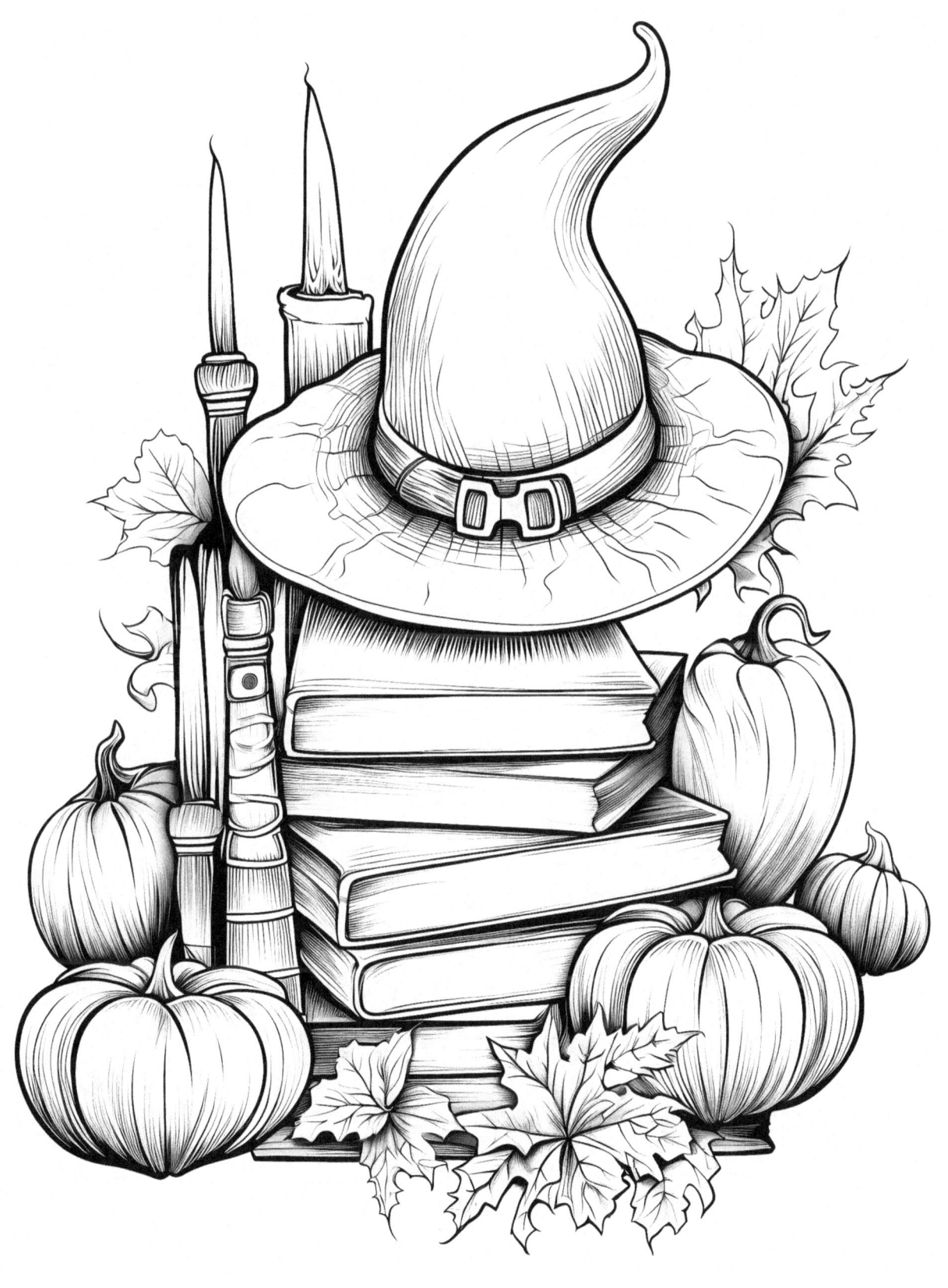

THANK YOU

FOR CHOOSING OUR COLORING BOOK!

Your support has made our day brighter and touched the hearts of everyone who contributed to this book.

♥

We hope this coloring book brings you immense joy and relaxation as you embark on this creative journey.

If you enjoyed our coloring book, please consider leaving us a review on Amazon. Your feedback helps other potential customers discover the value of our work and also serves as a source of inspiration for our ongoing endeavors.

Connect with us on social media for an exclusive peek into the captivating interiors of our coloring books and journals, essential updates, and a vibrant community vibe.

- TIKTOK: @creativetherapyhub
- INSTAGRAM: @creativetherapyhub
- FACEBOOK: creativetherapyhub
- YOUTUBE: Creative Therapy Hub

Also, if you'd like to share your thoughts on future projects, please write to us, and we will happily hear you out.
Let's create, connect, and inspire together! See you there! ♥

COPYRIGHT ©2023 Creative Therapy Hub. All rights reserved.

The reproduction, distribution, or transmission of any part of this material in any form without the prior written consent of the publisher is strictly prohibited. Only incorporating brief excerpts into critical reviews is allowed.

GUIDELINES FOR USING THIS BOOK

Our paper selection is of standard quality to ensure affordability, given the limited paper options available on Amazon. We suggest placing a thick sheet of paper behind the page you are working on to prevent any potential bleeding onto the following pages caused by specific pens or markers.

CREATIVE COLORING TIPS

1. Begin with gentle strokes and progressively layer the colors to achieve your desired intensity. This technique empowers you to manage saturation and prevent the initial color application from becoming overly dark.

2. Experiment with blending colors by layering different shades on each other. Use pencils with similar tones to create smooth transitions.

3. Test new colors on the Test Color Page before applying them to your main artwork. It helps you see how the colors interact and whether they match your vision.

4. Experiment with different approaches, such as shading, cross-hatching, and stippling, to infuse your coloring with dimension and texture.

5. Sort your pencils or markers by color families to find the shades you need to stay organized.

6. Don't hesitate to experiment with unconventional color combinations. Unique color schemes can bring creativity to your artwork.

TEST COLOR PAGE

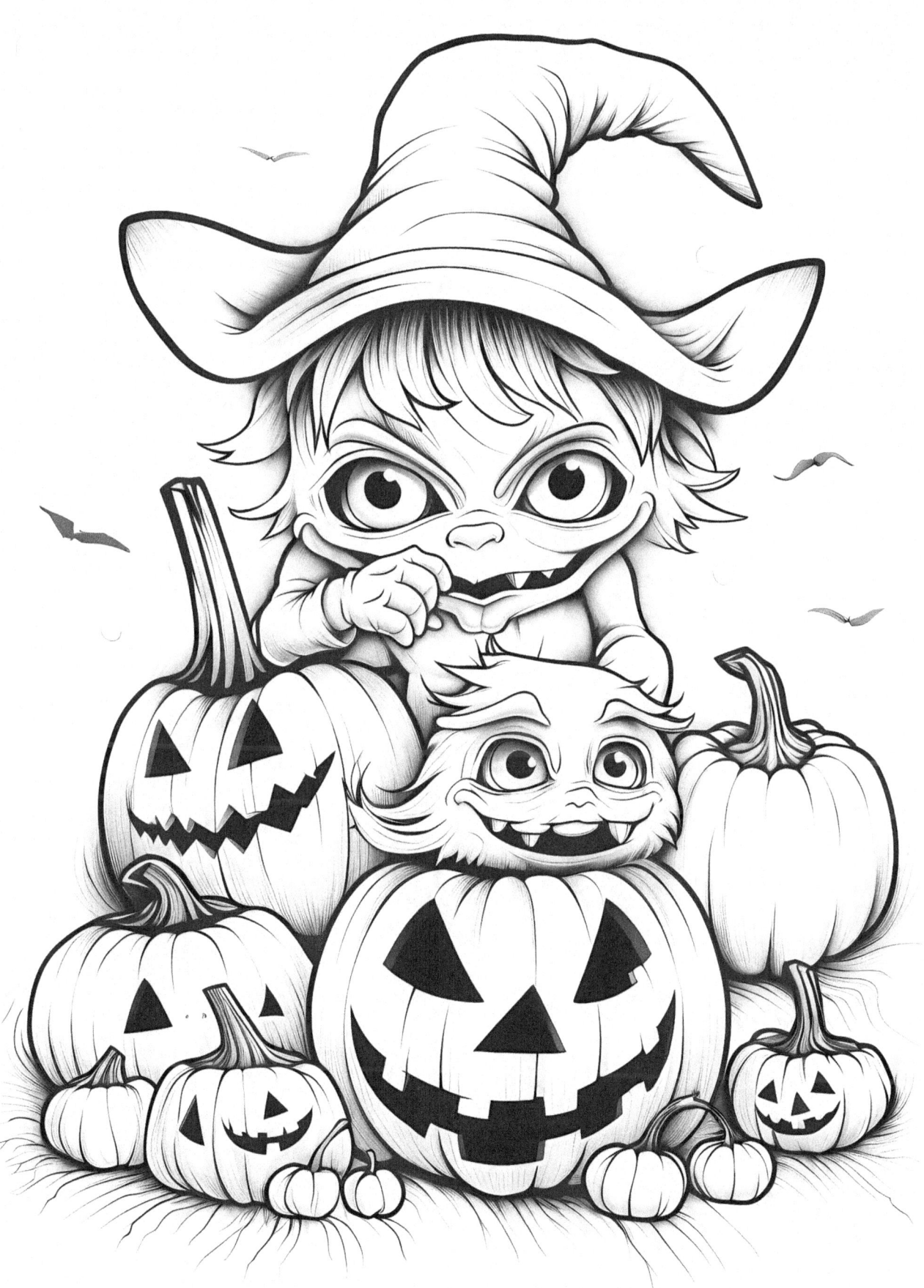

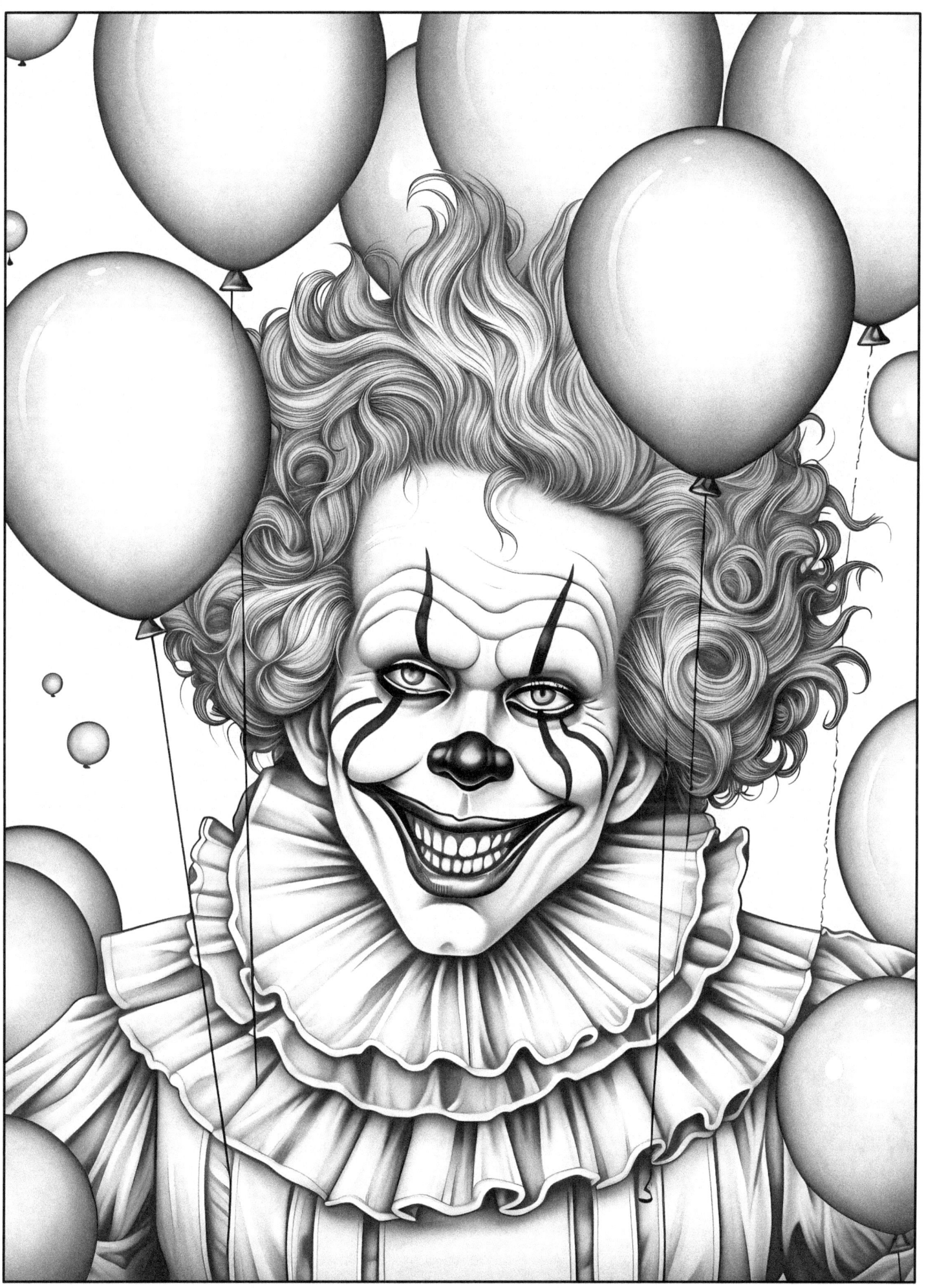

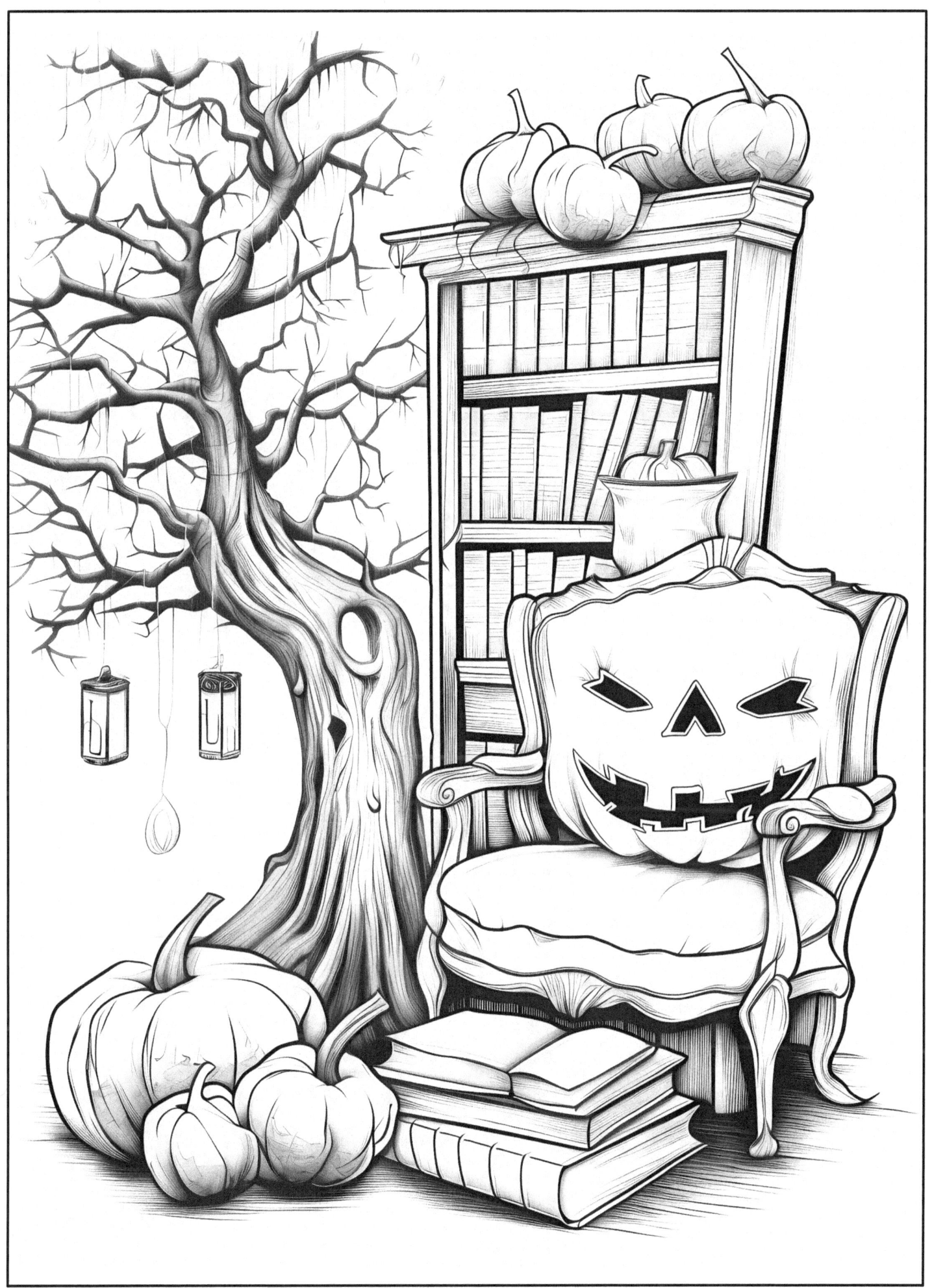

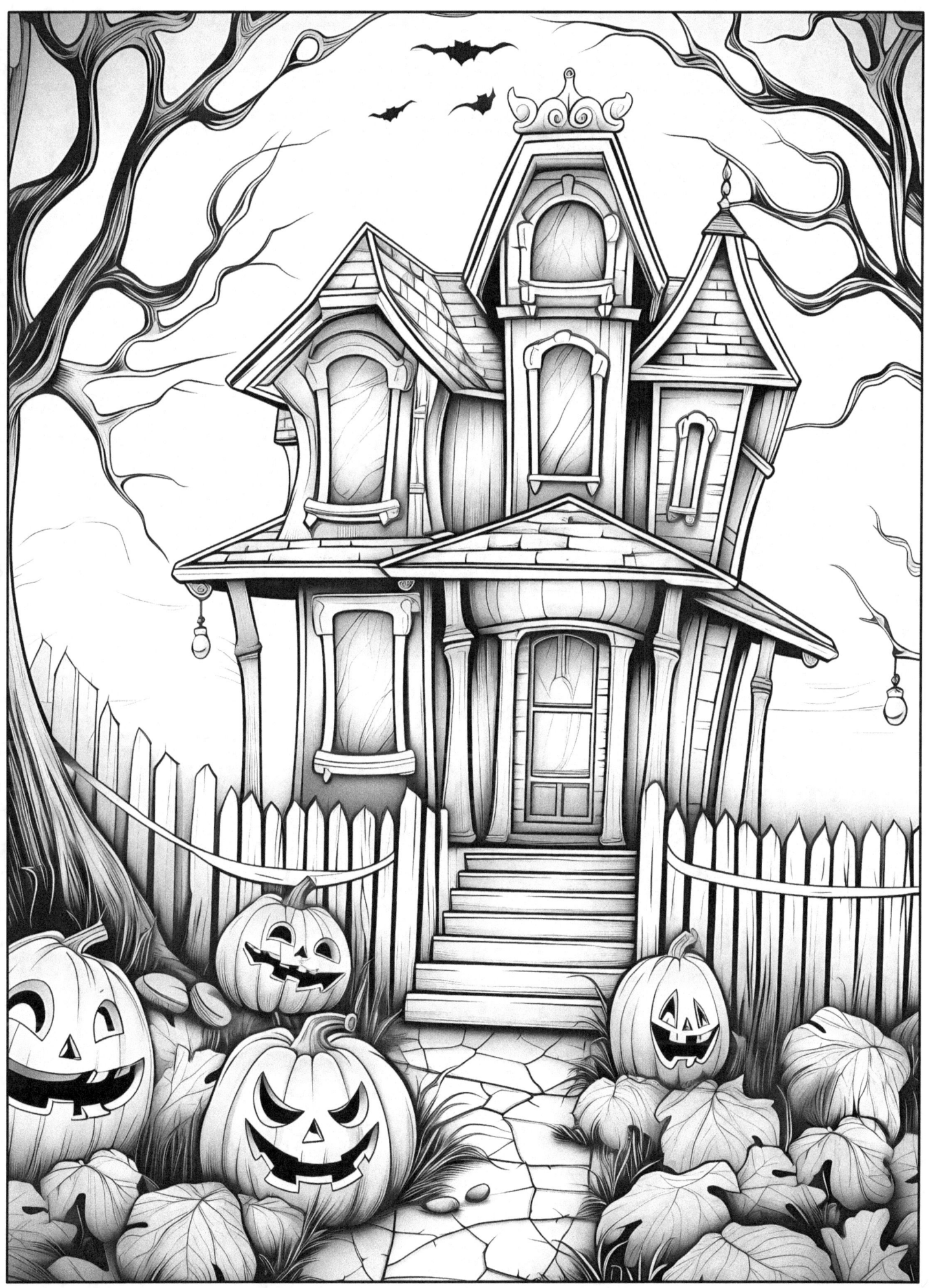

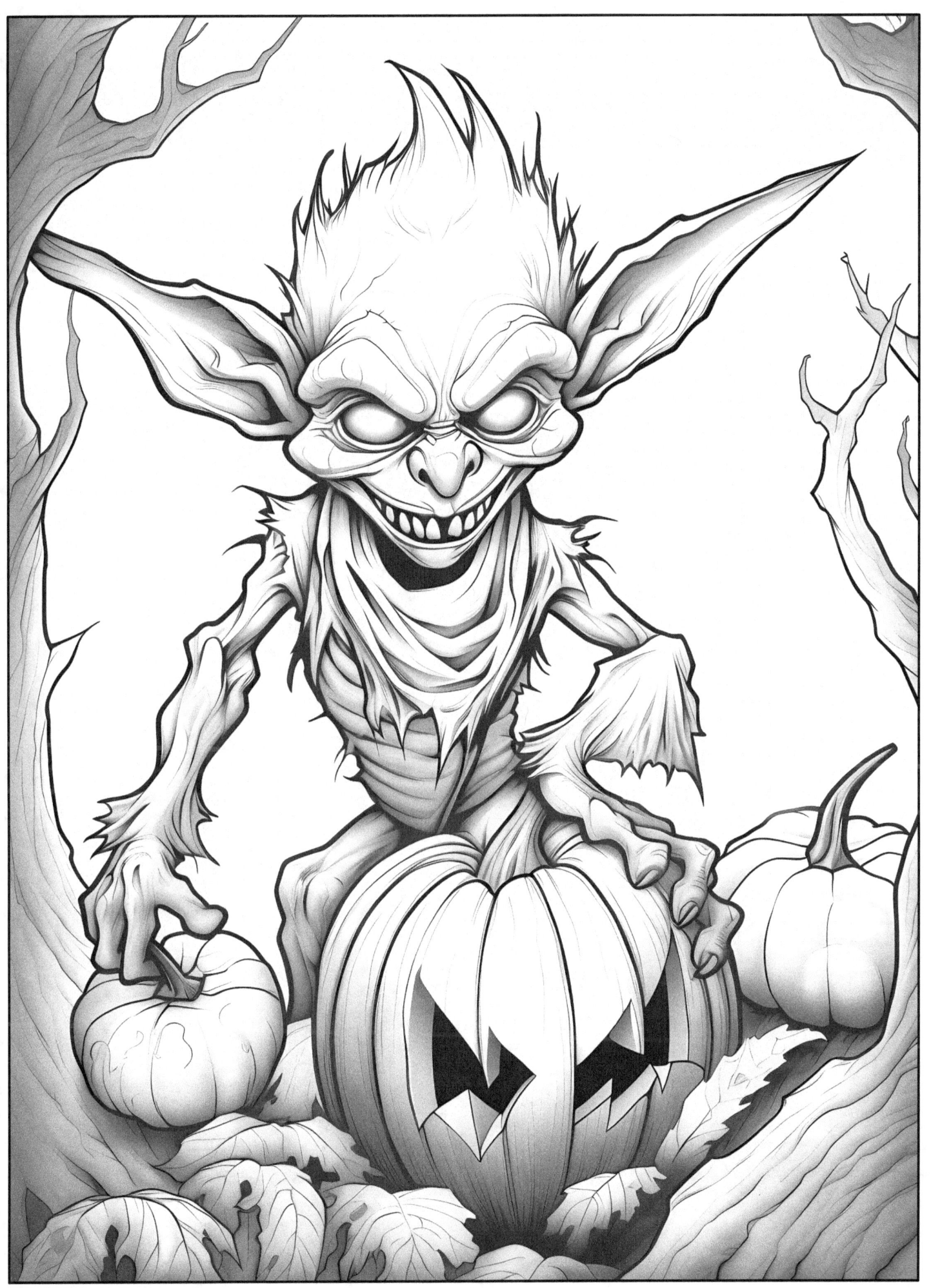

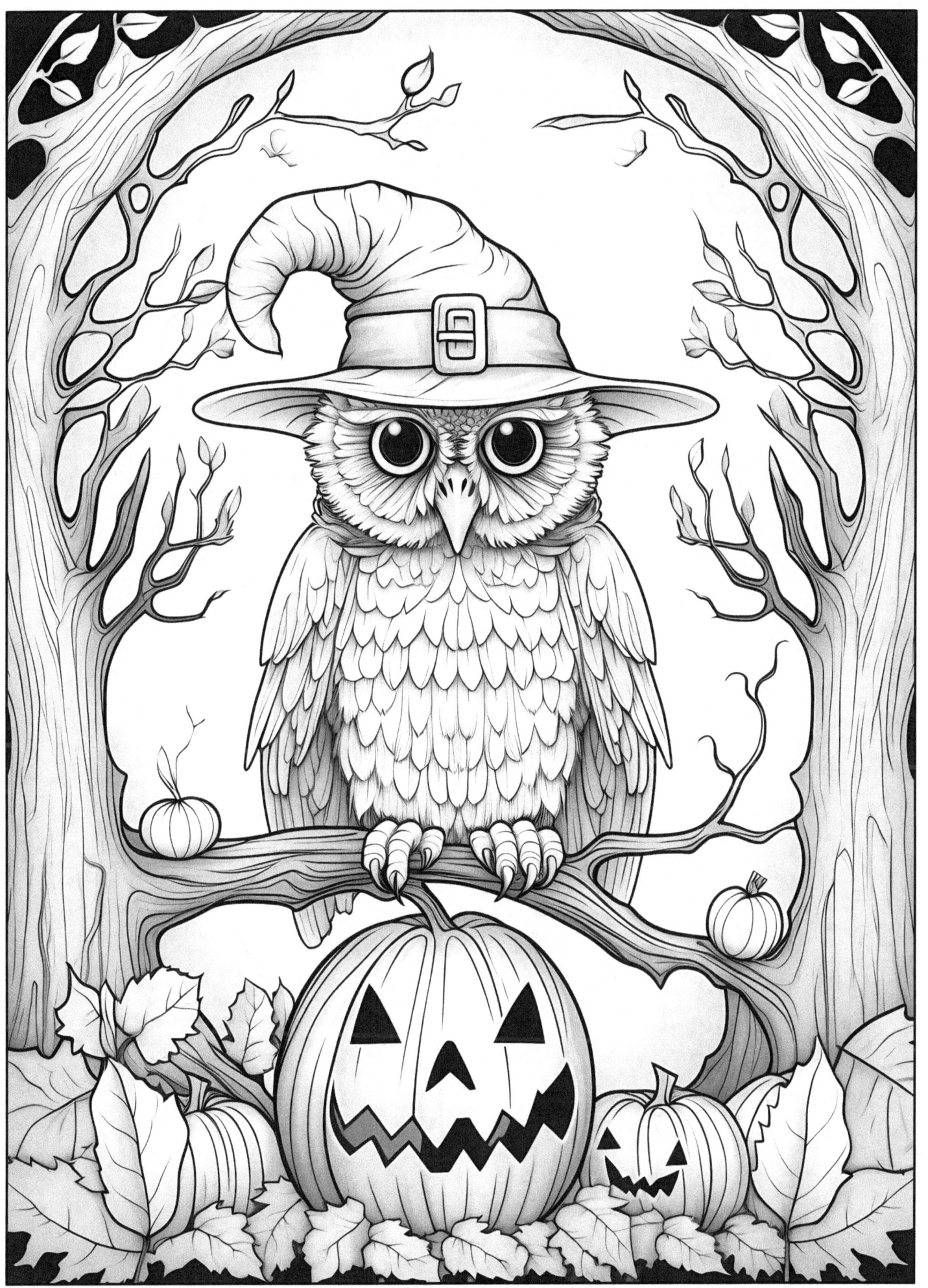

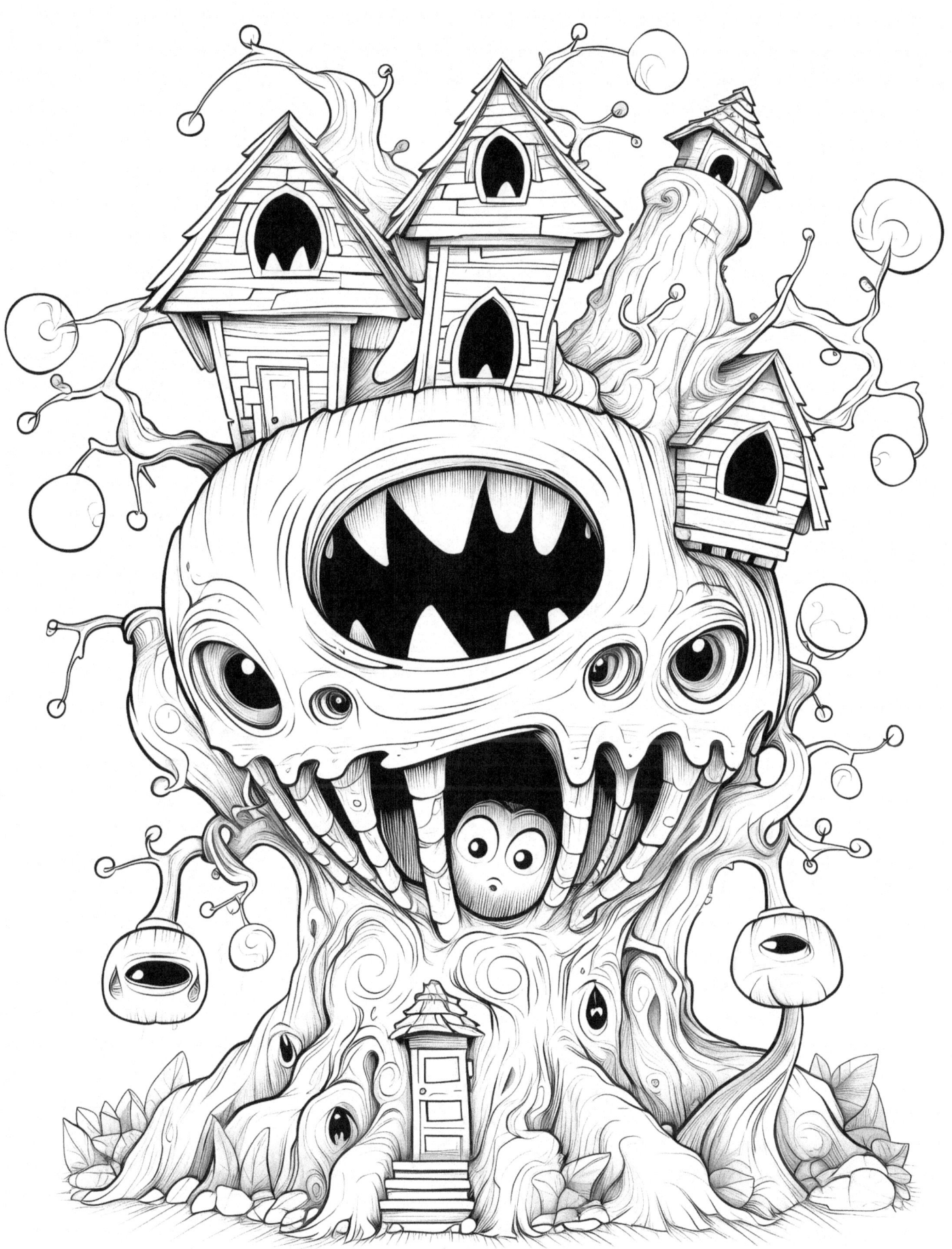

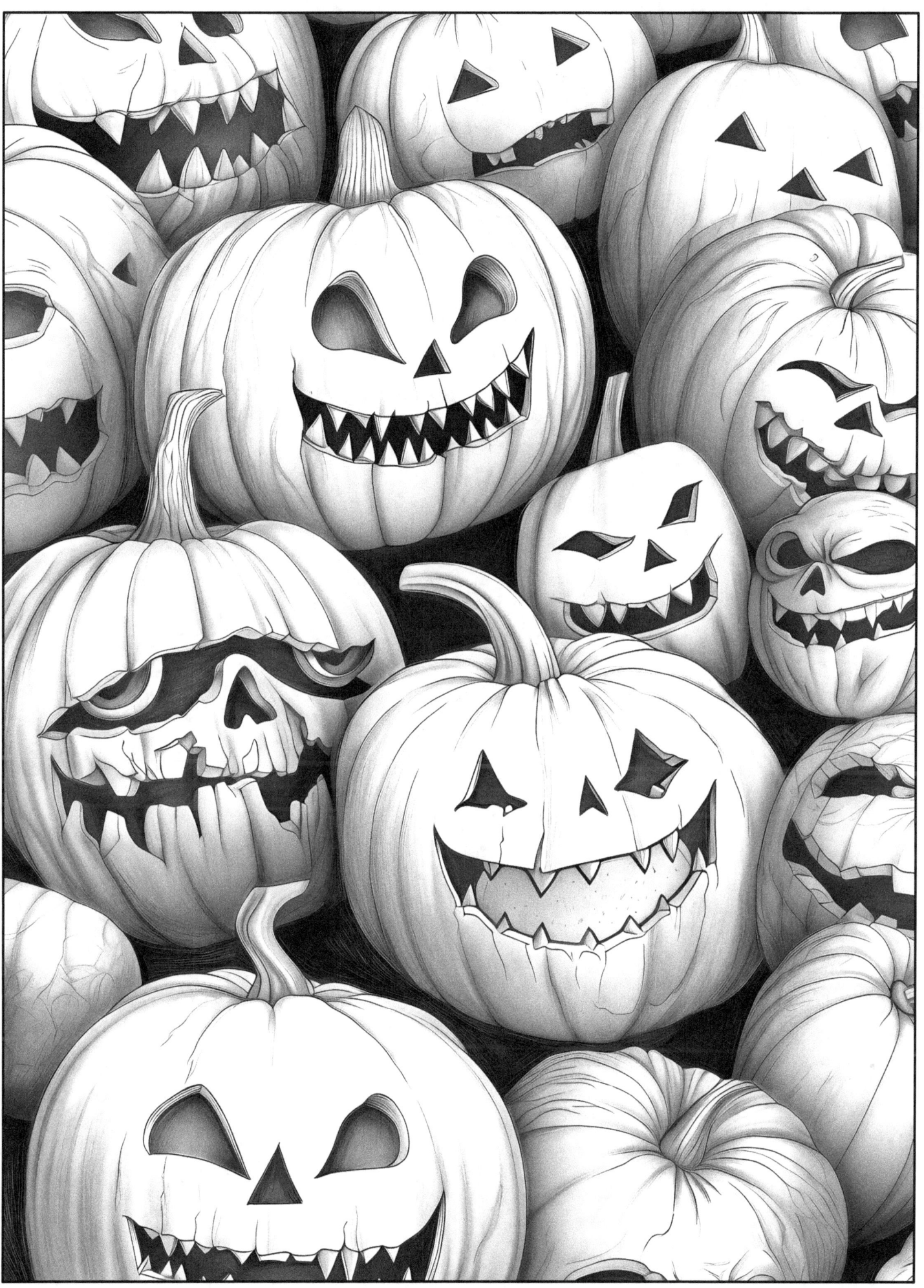

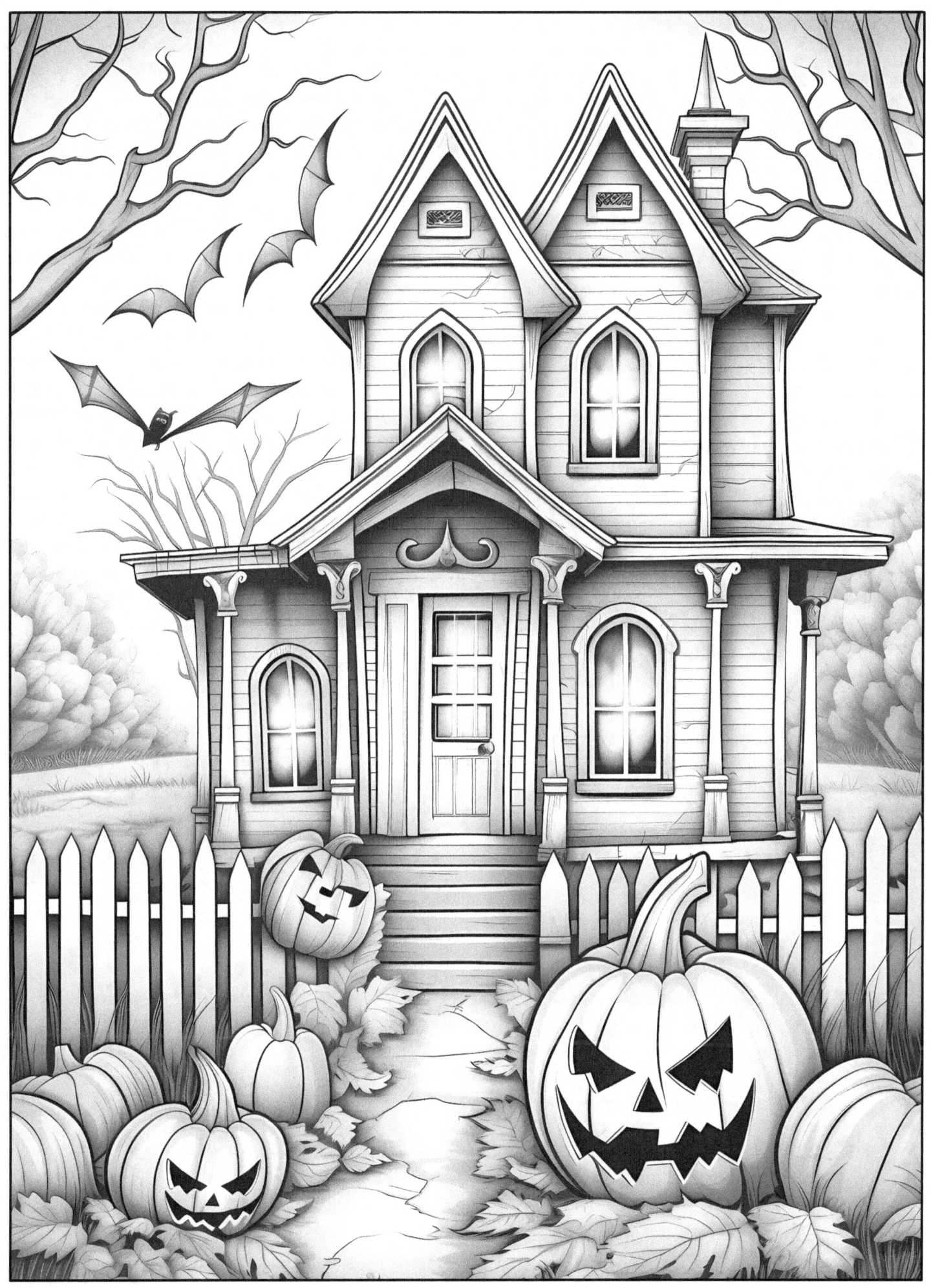

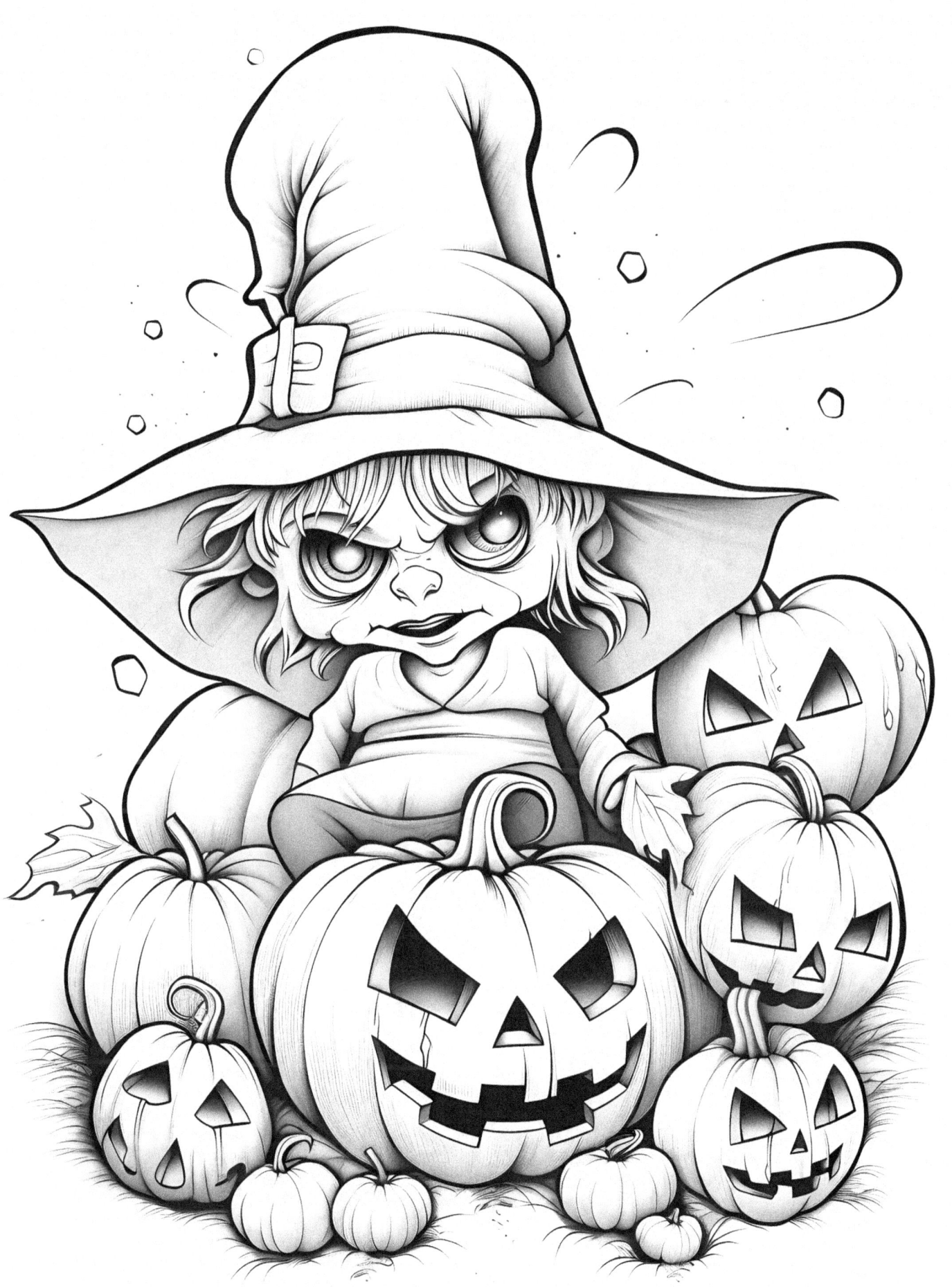

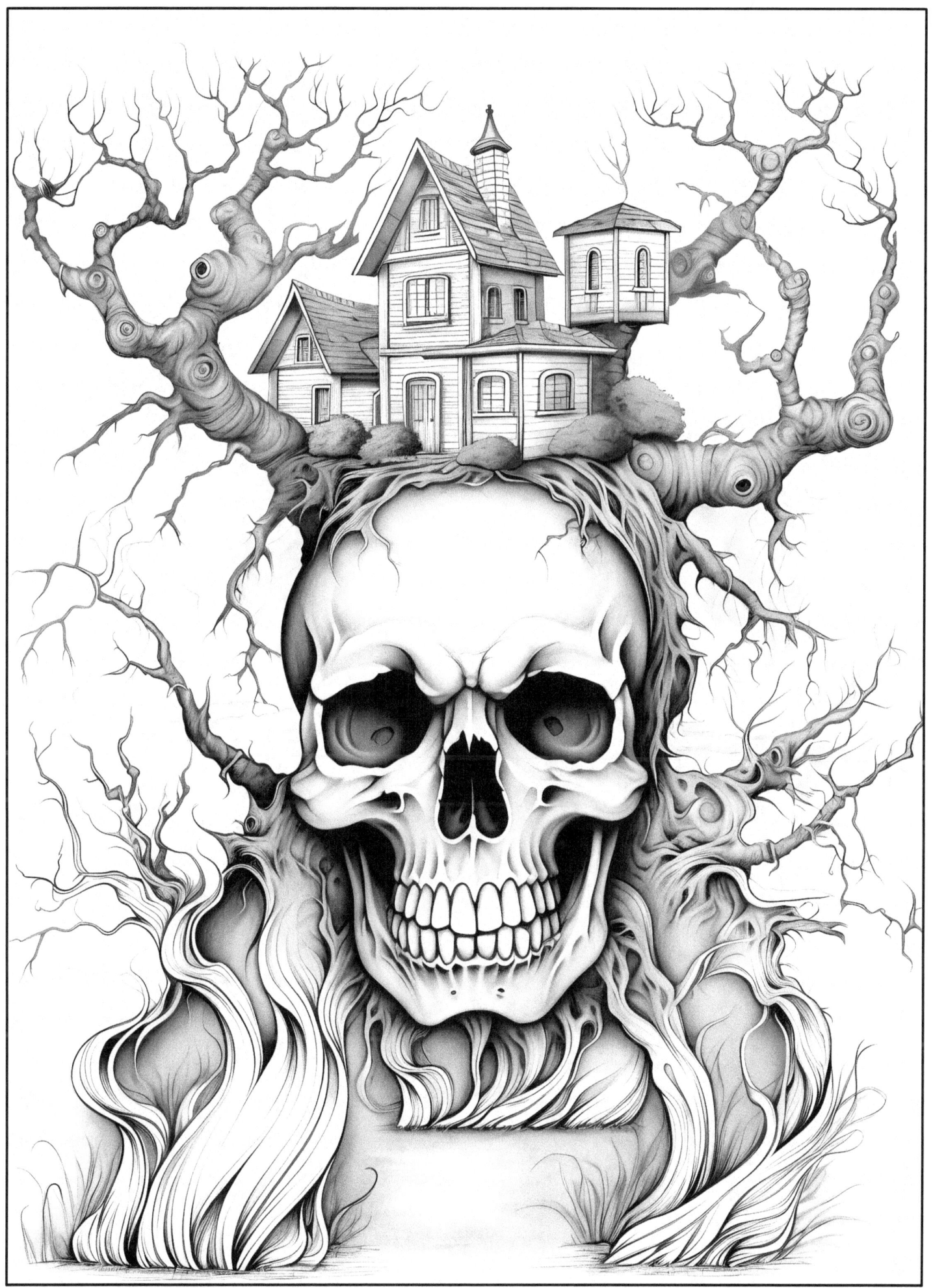

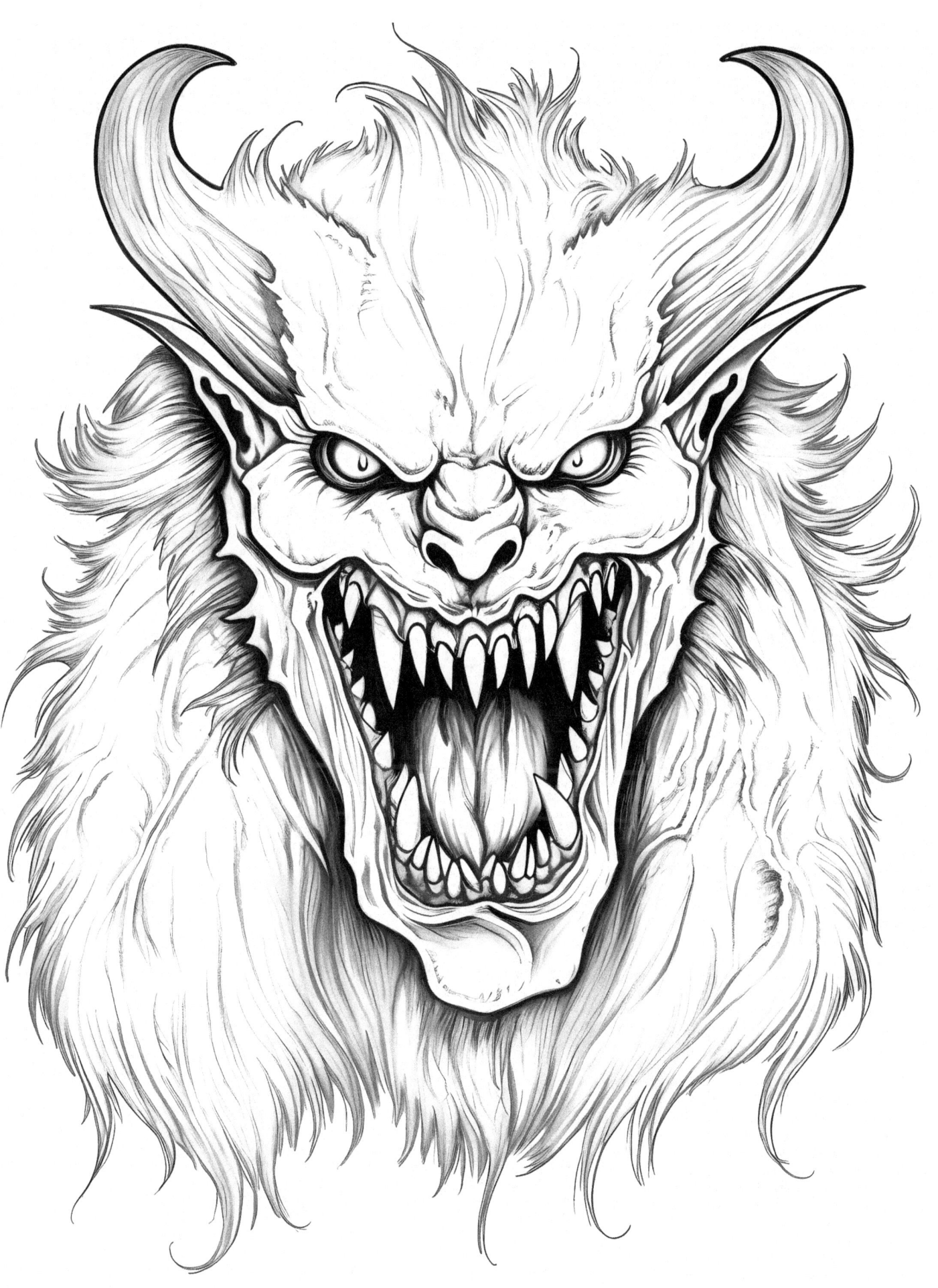

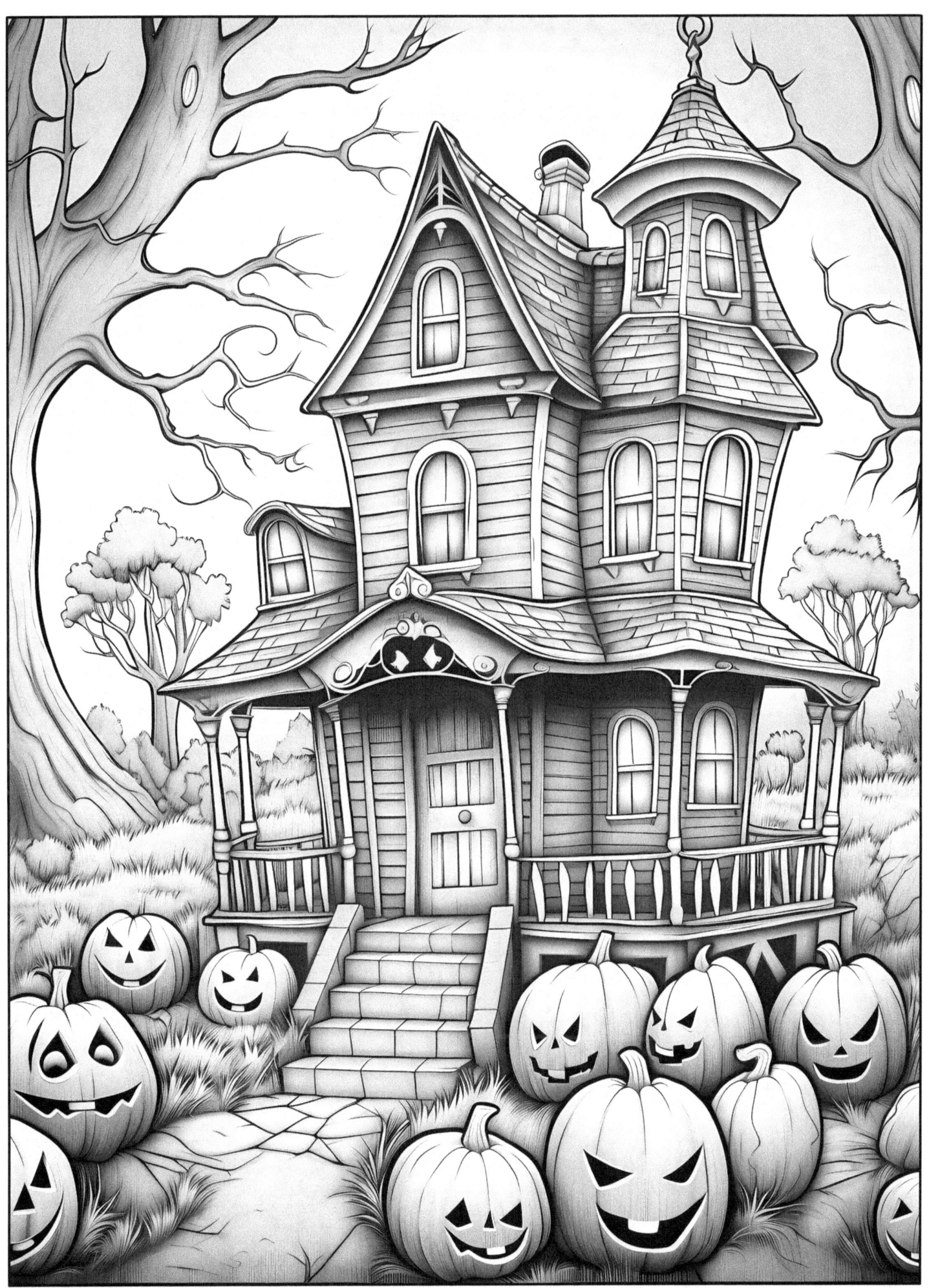

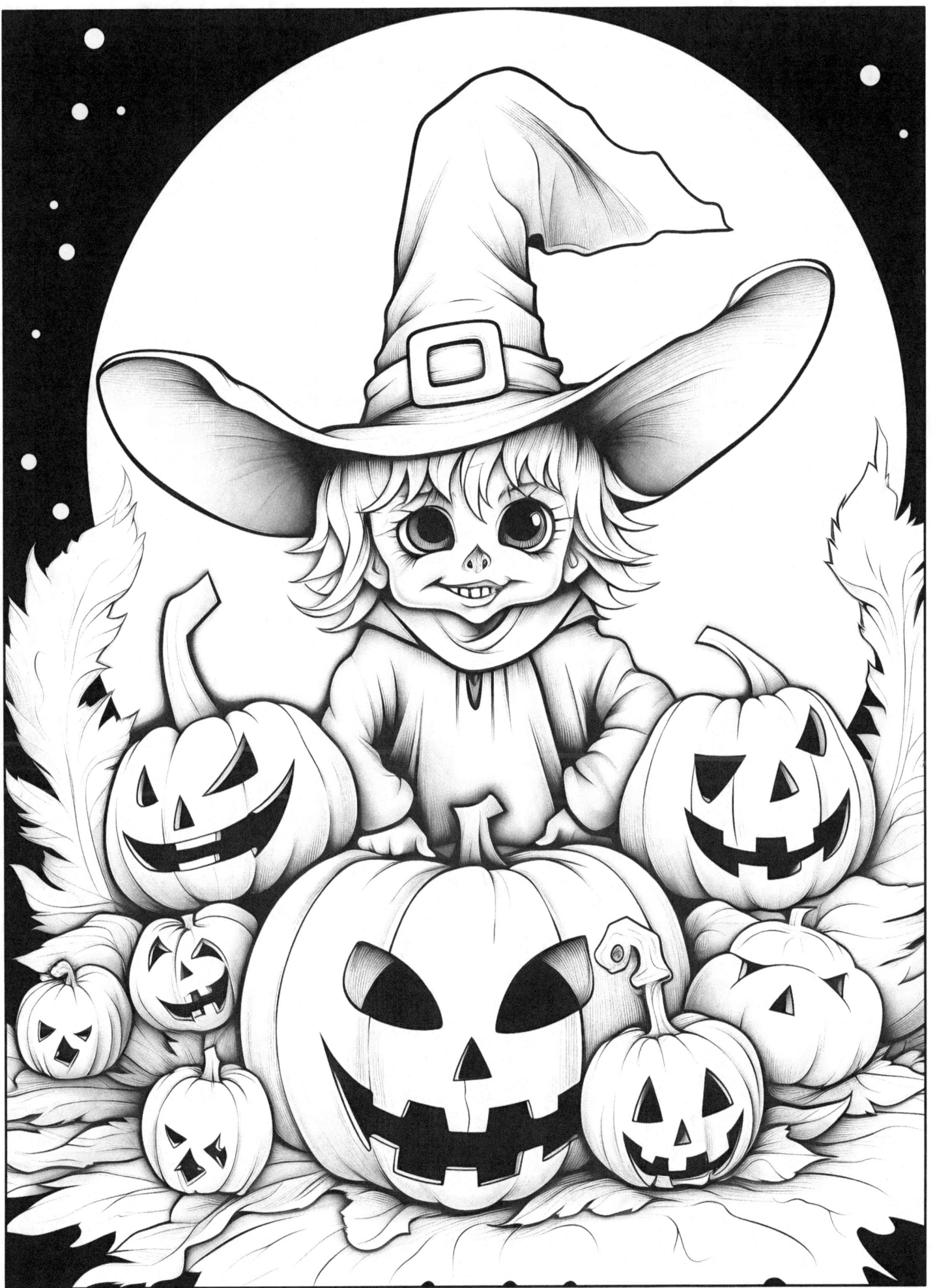

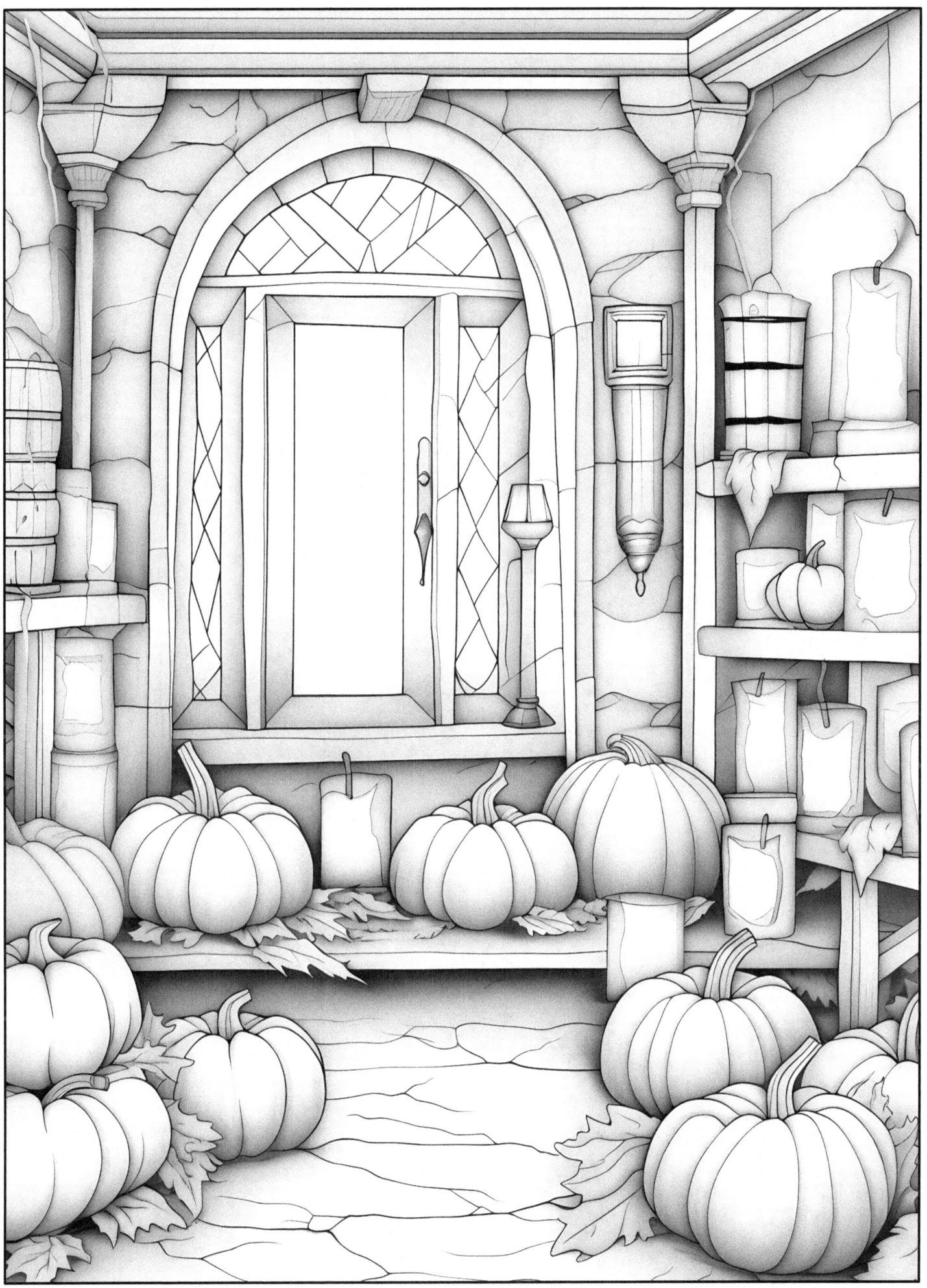

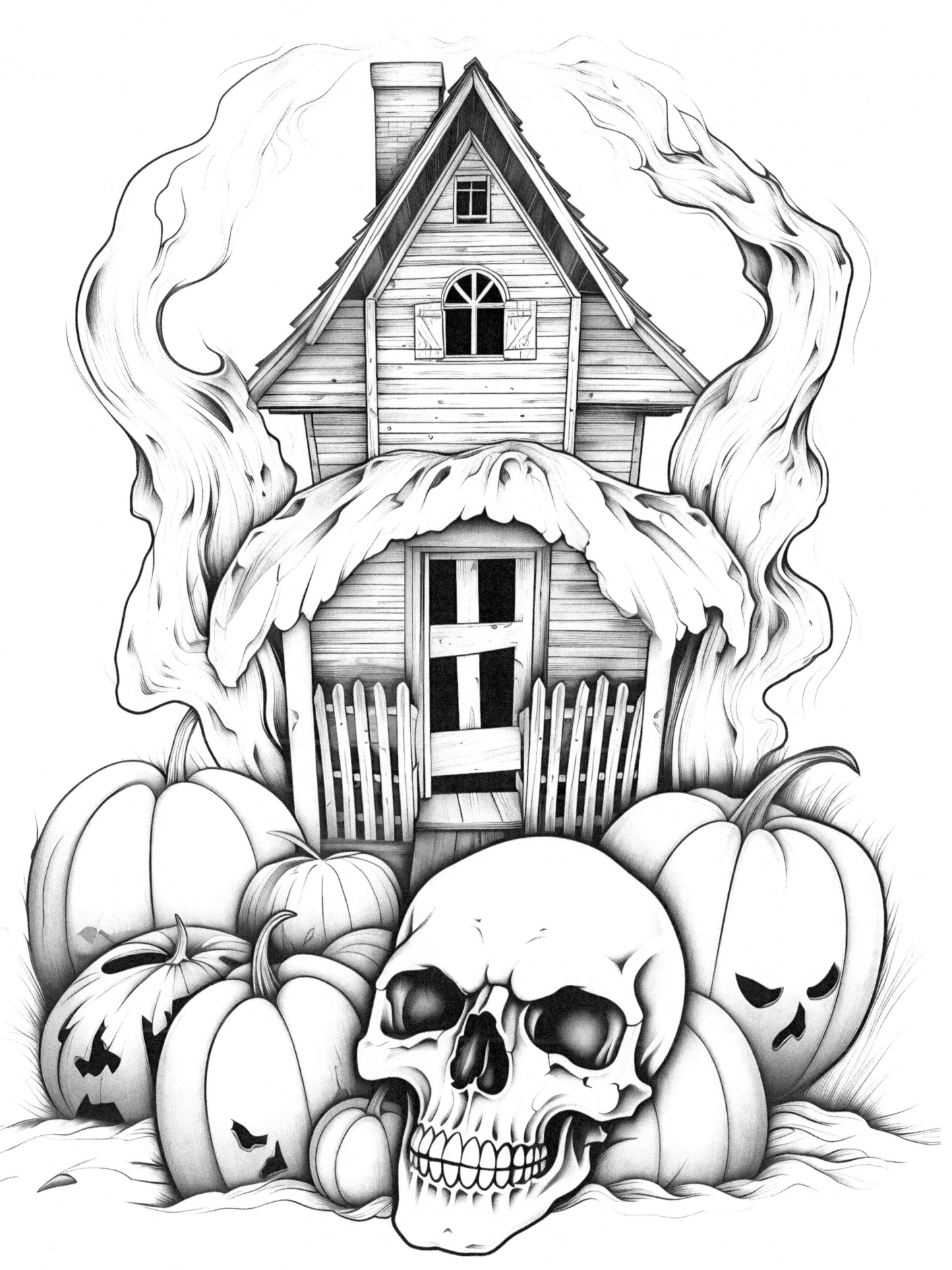

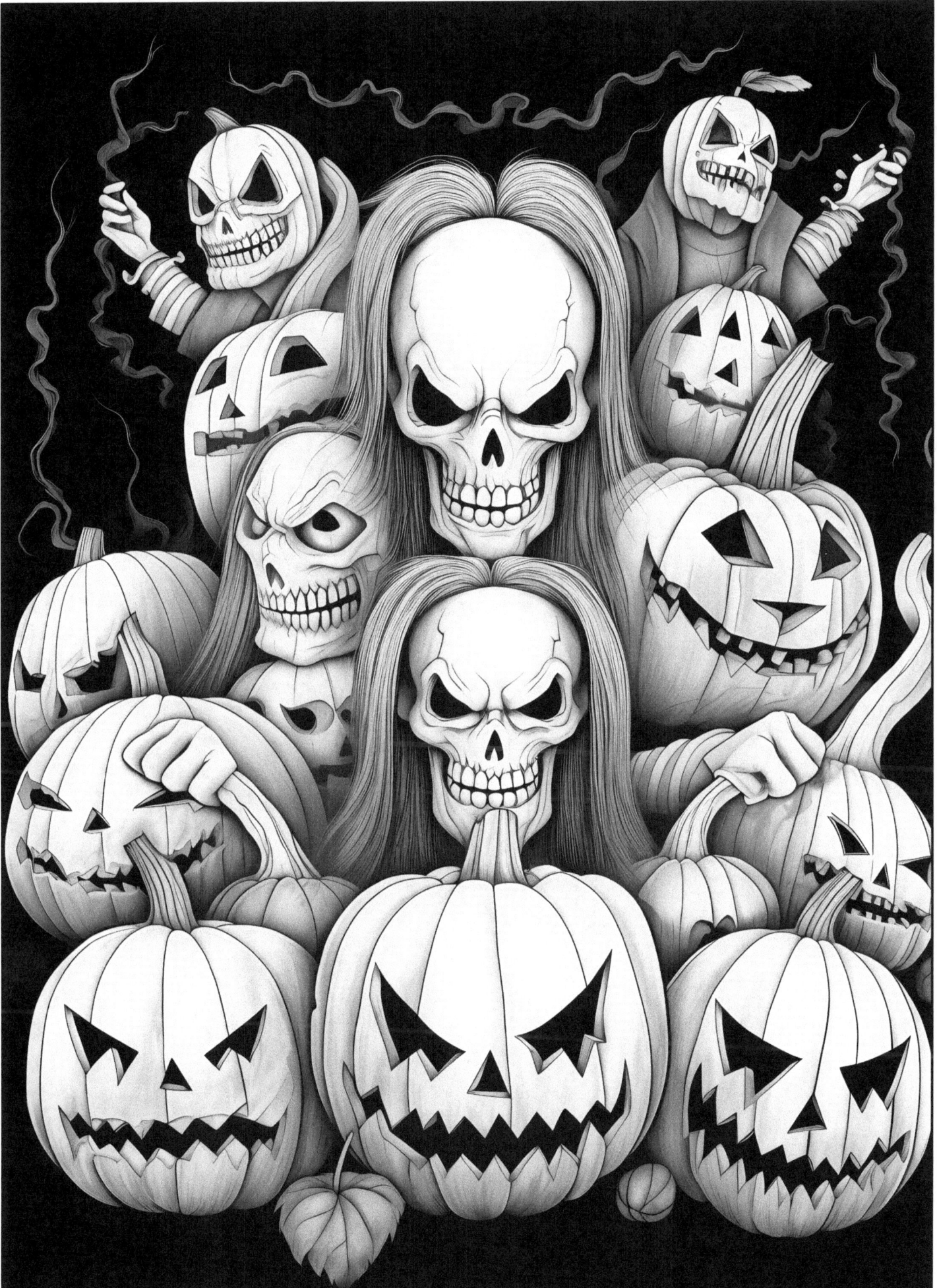

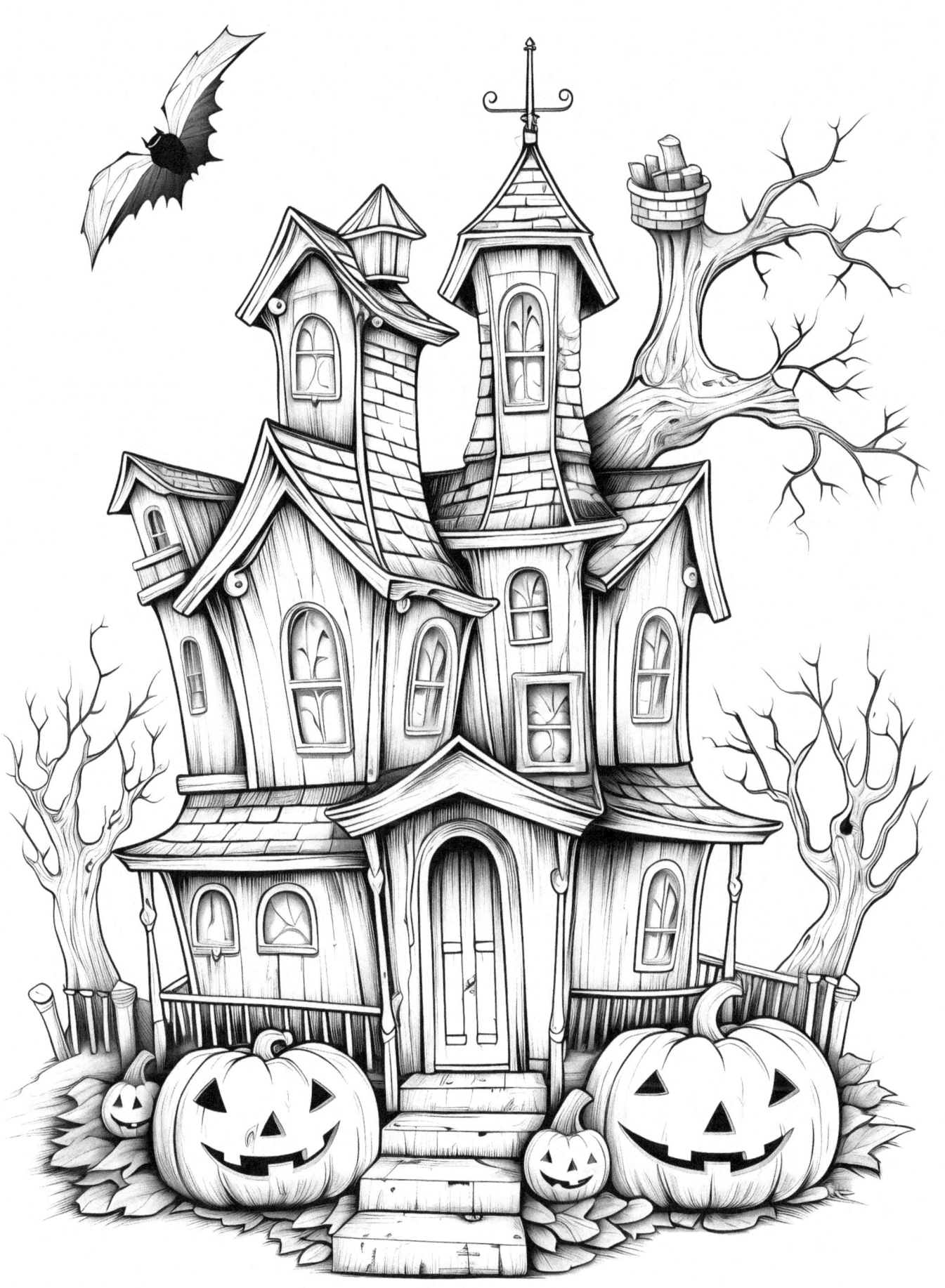

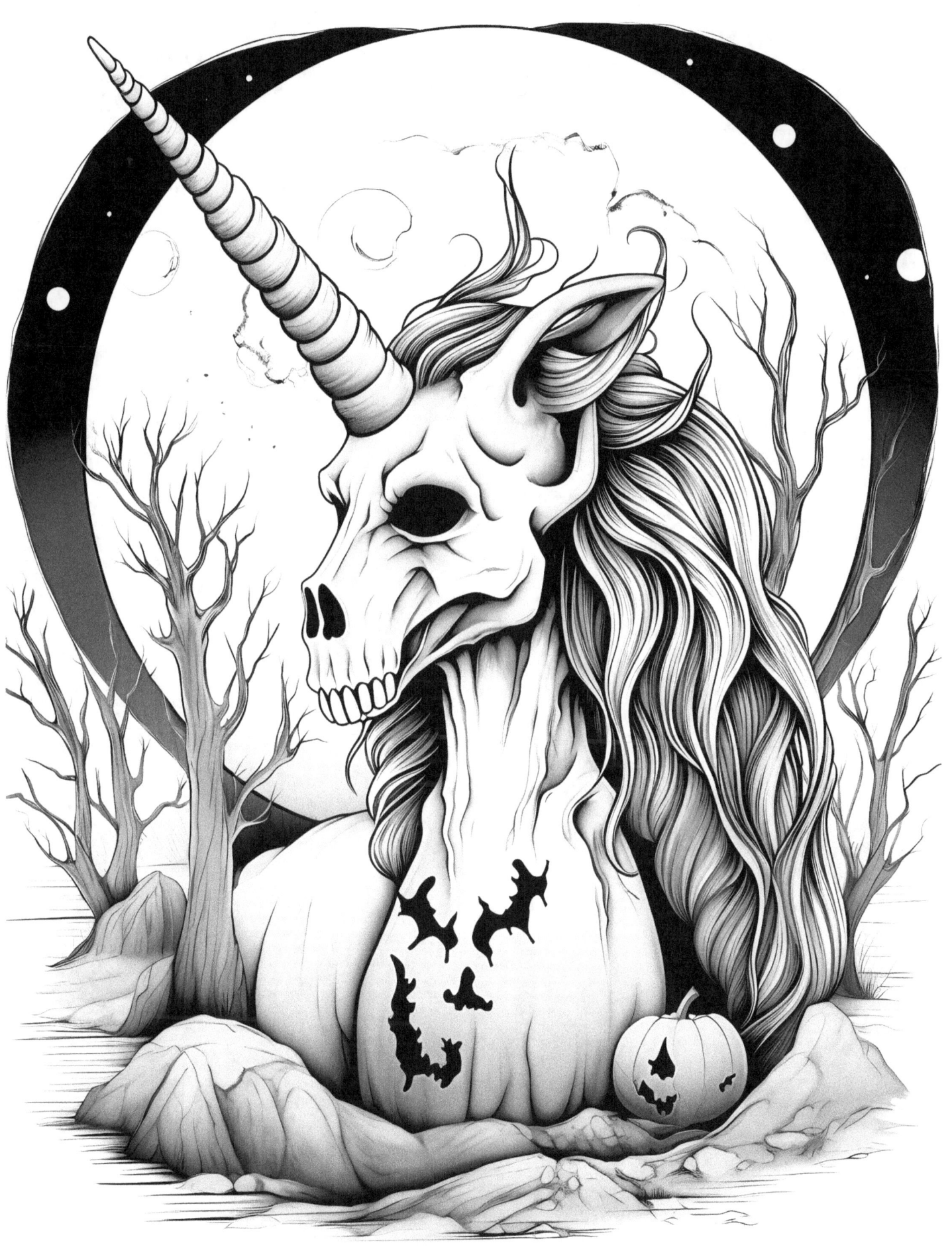

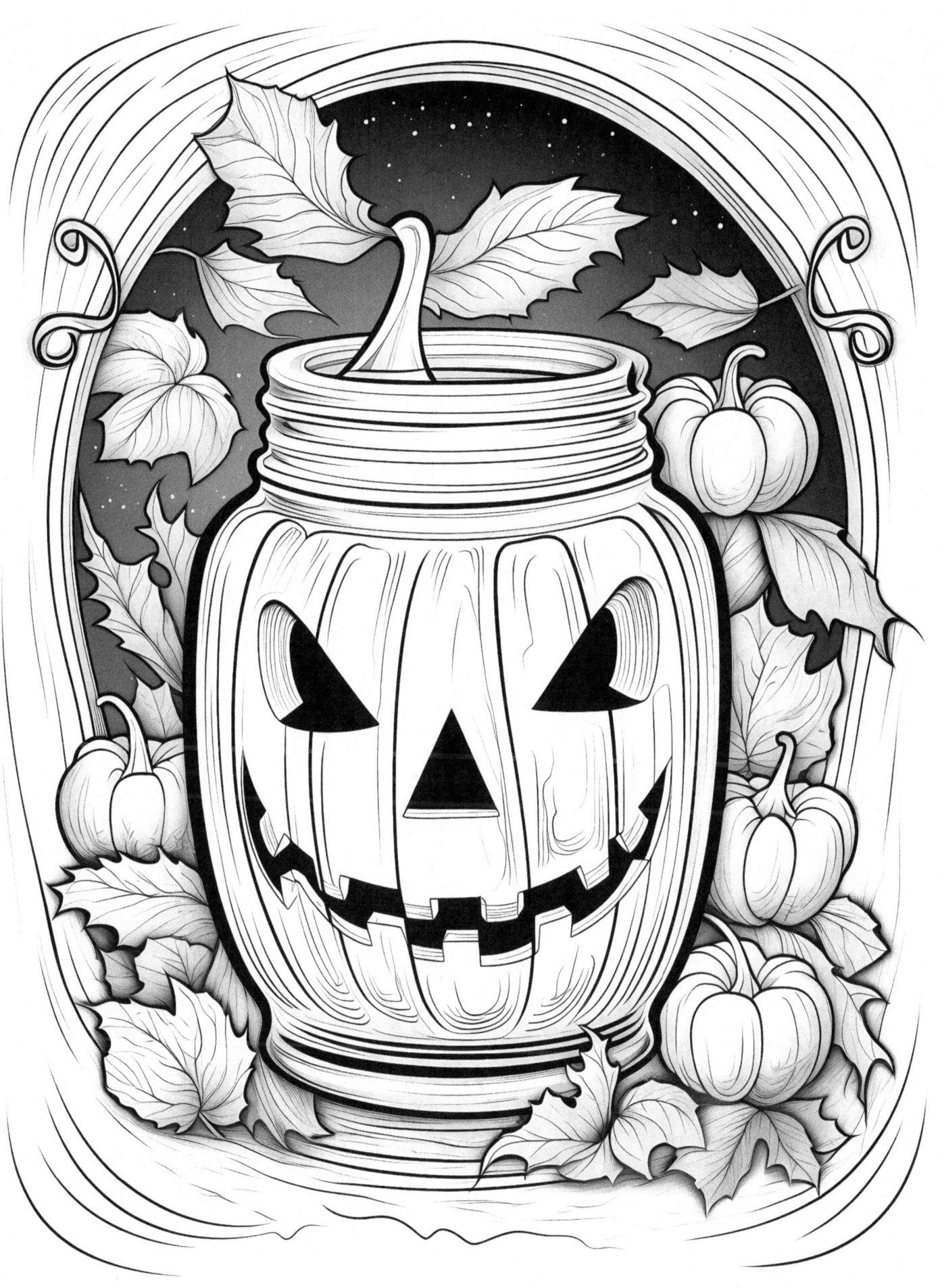

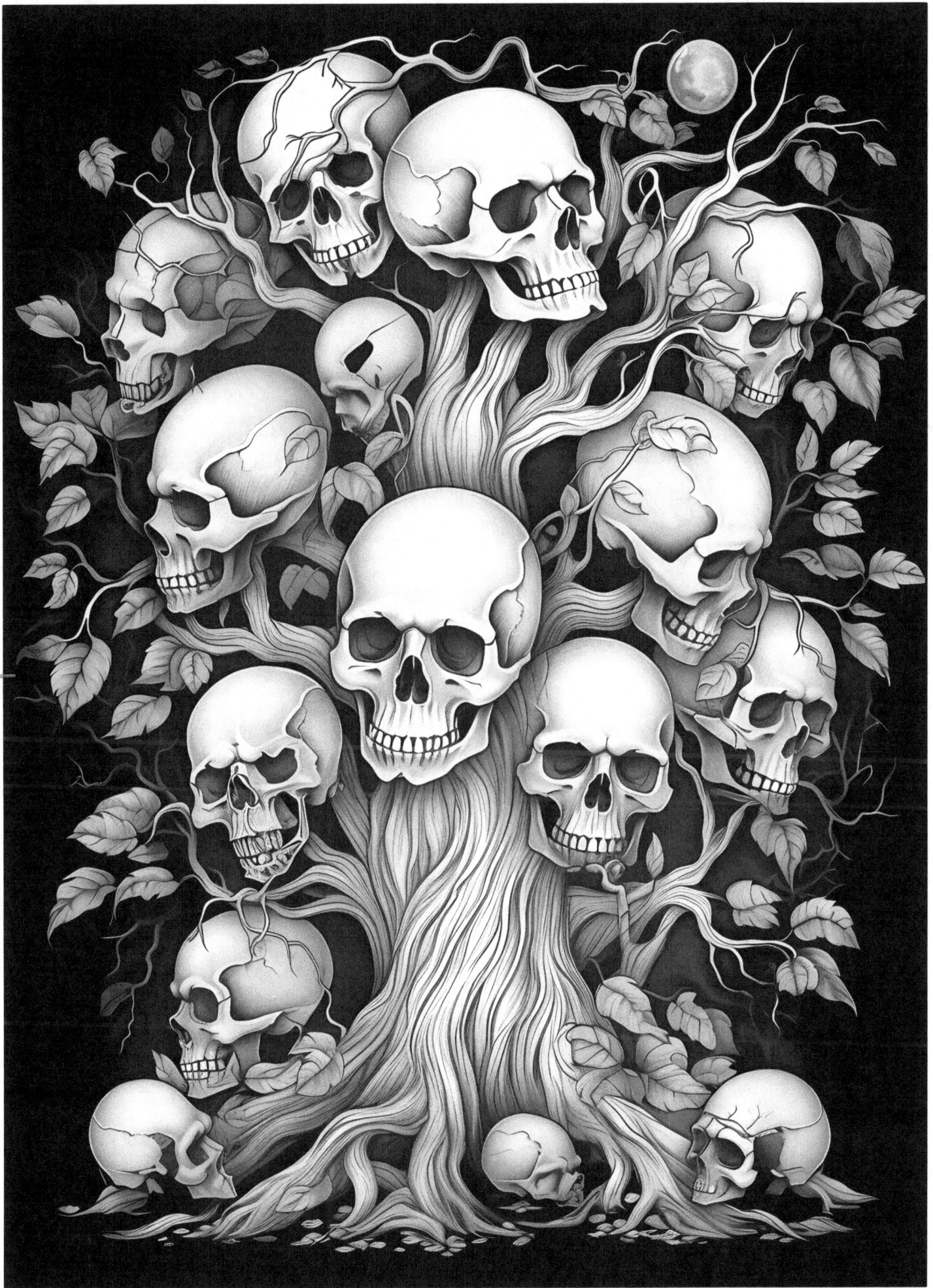

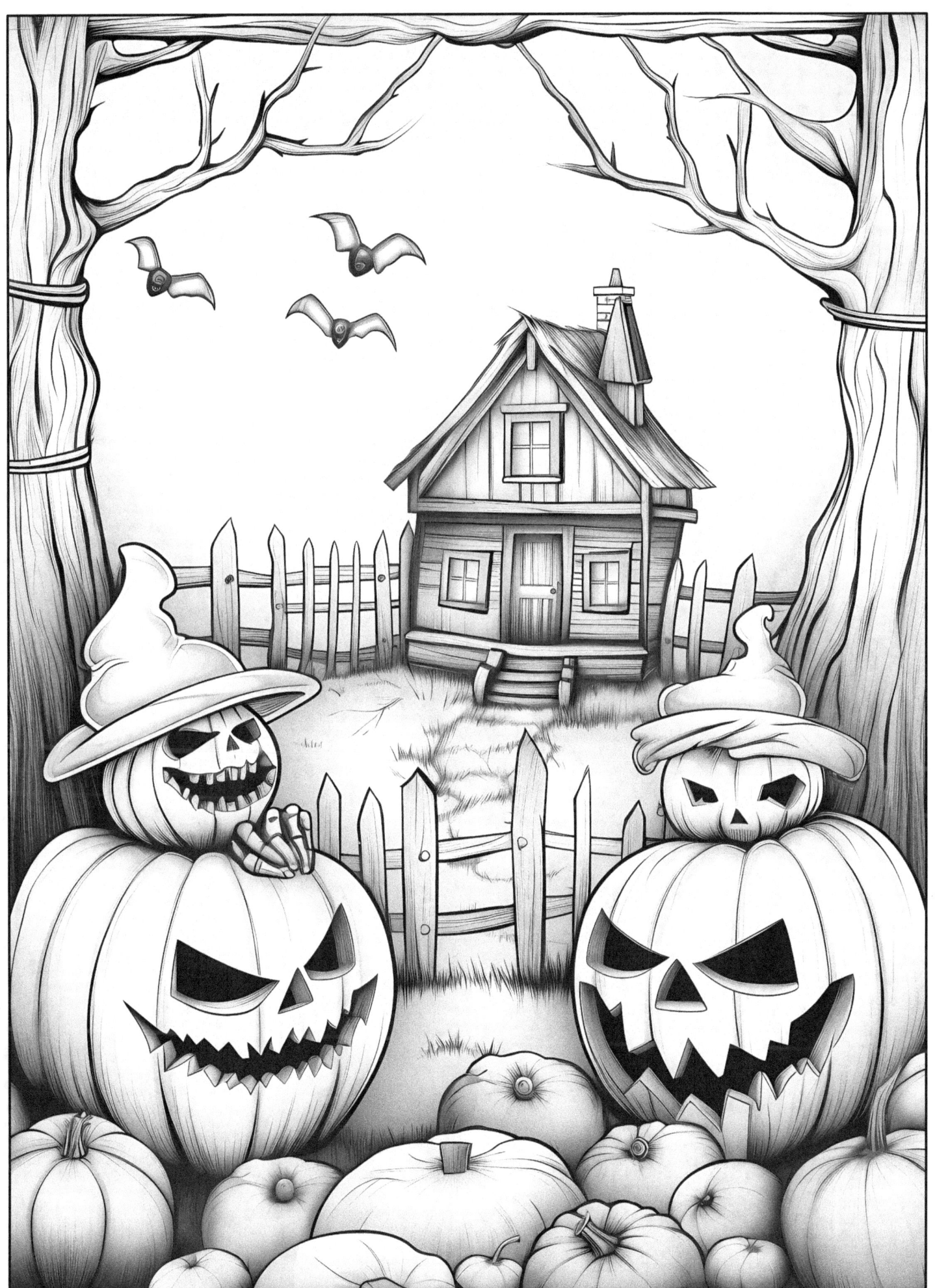

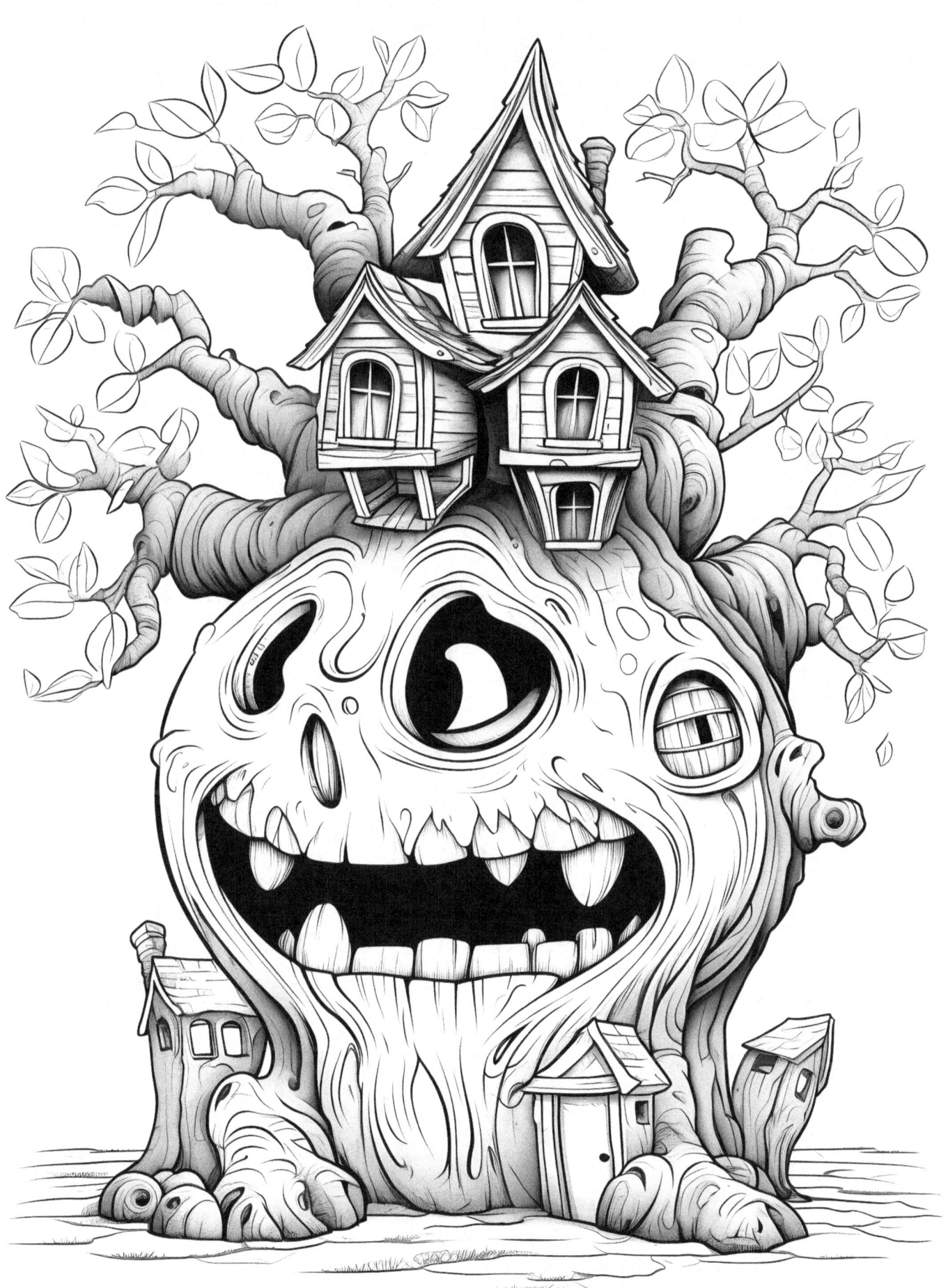

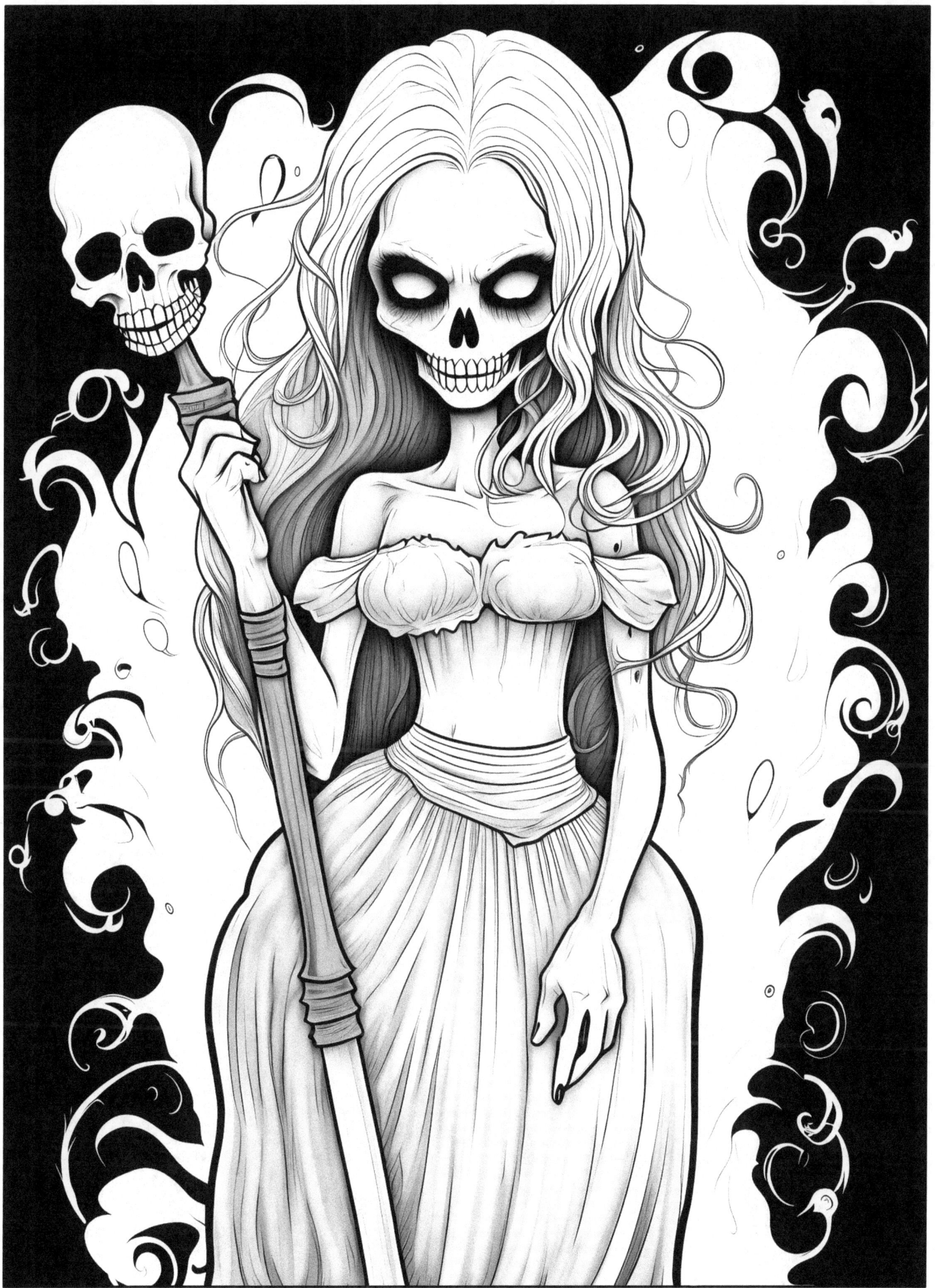

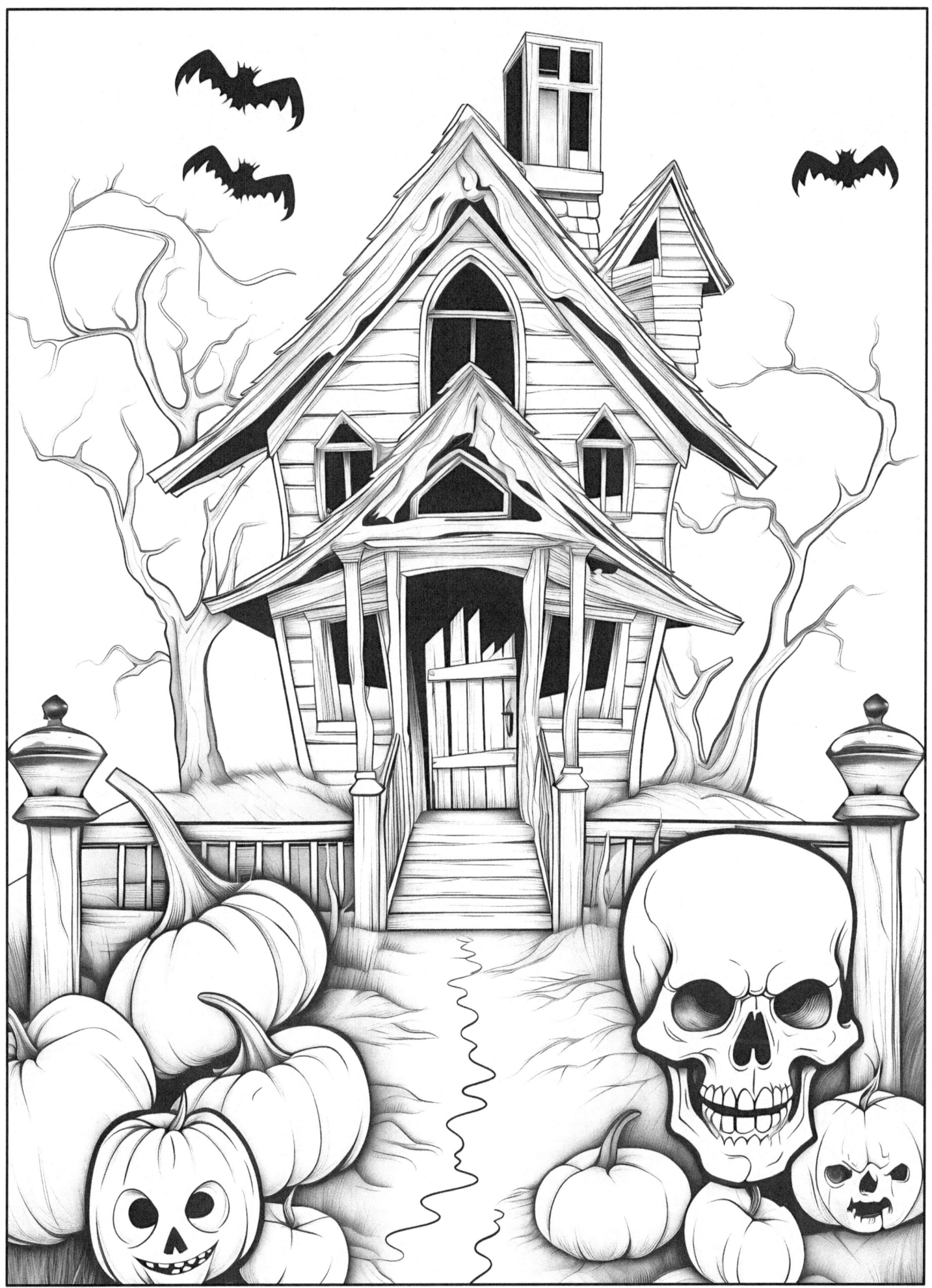

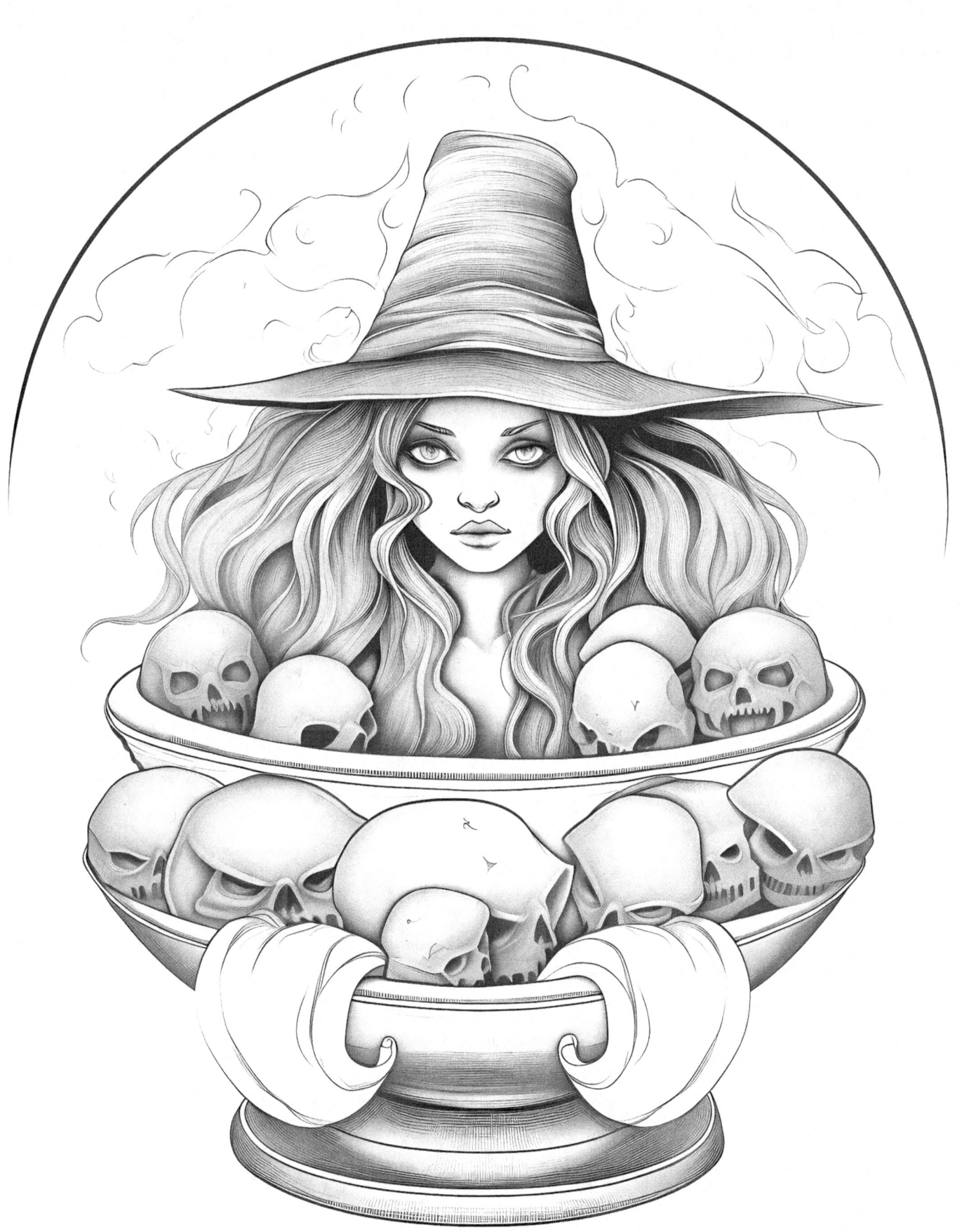

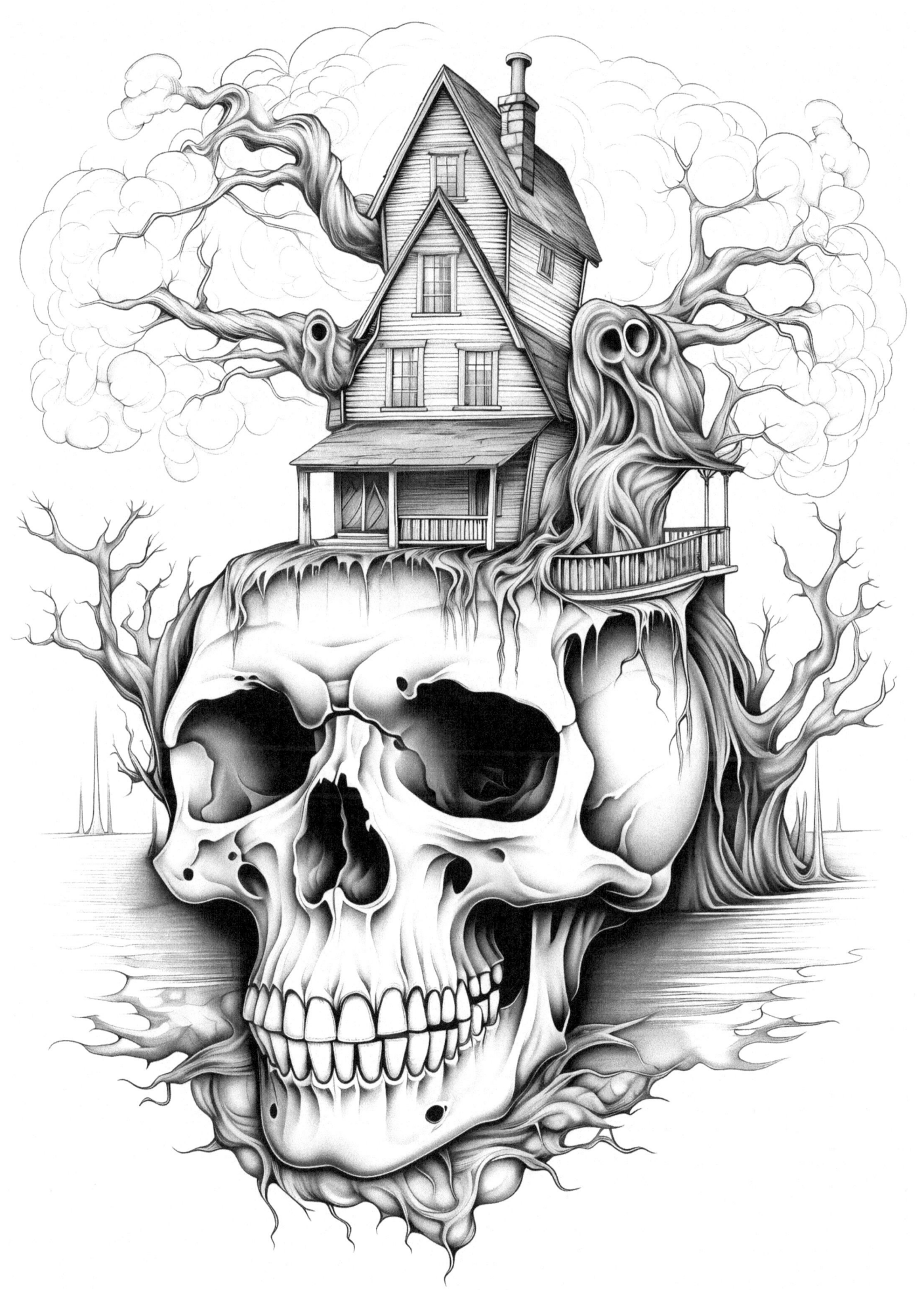

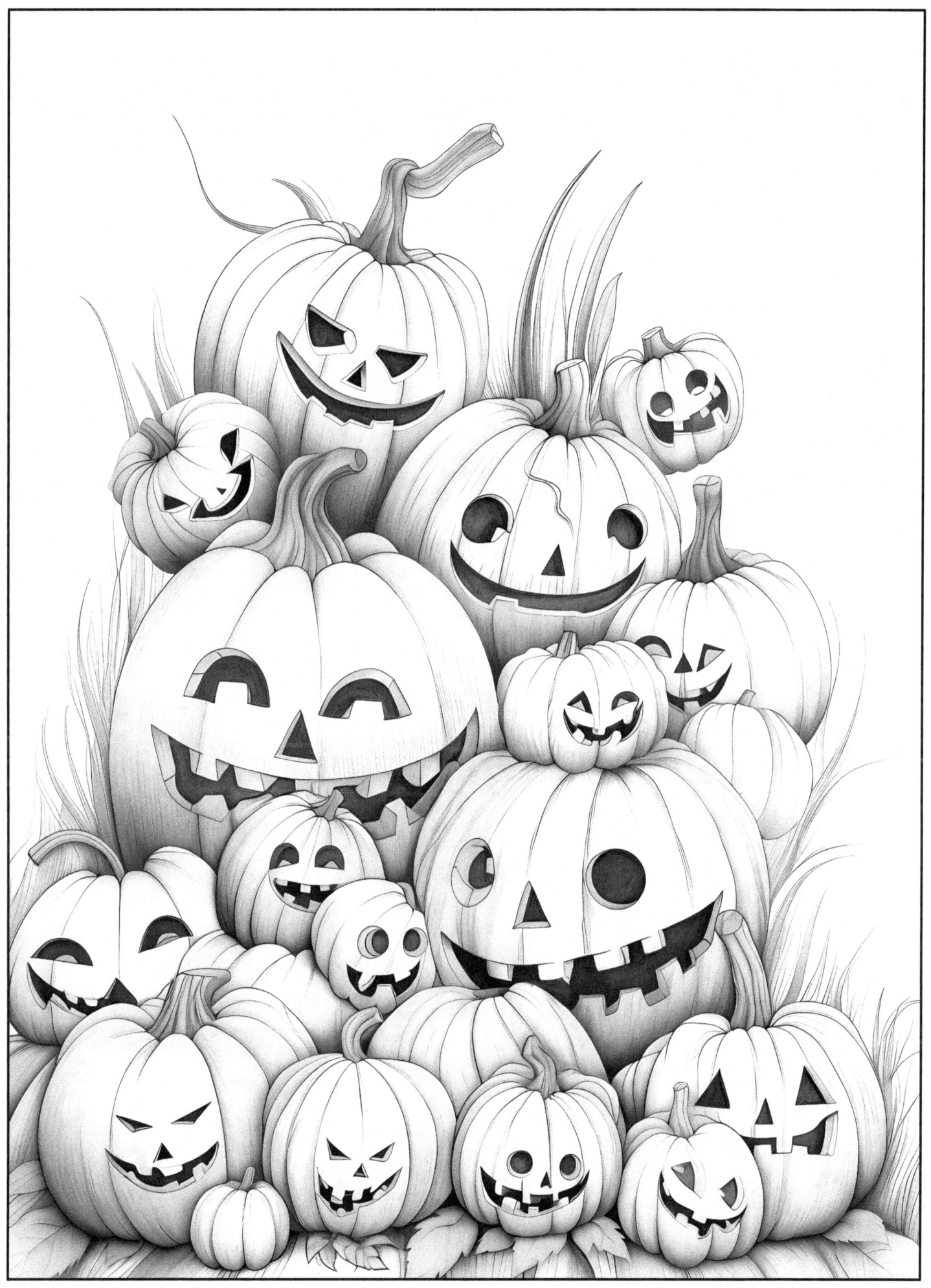

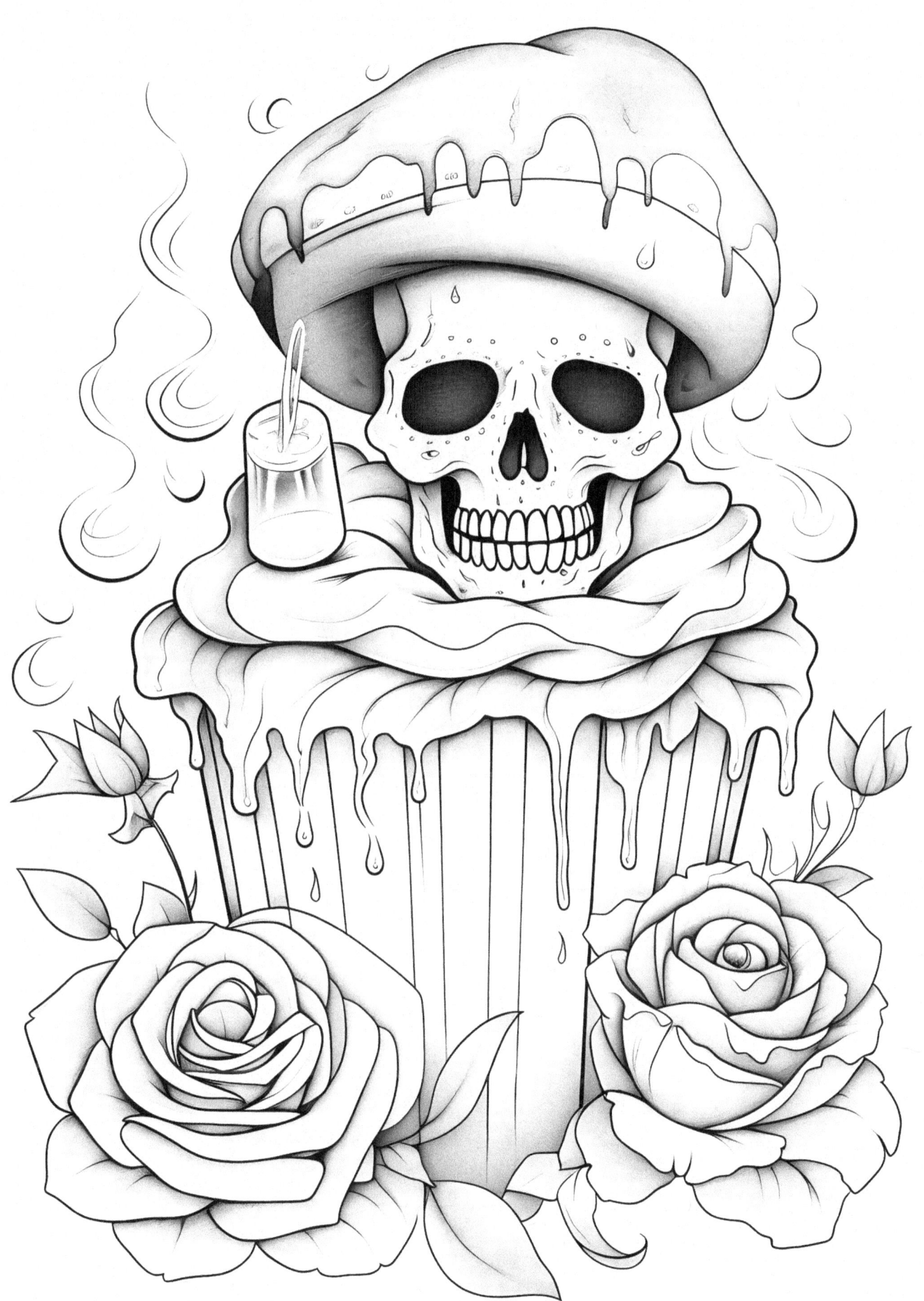

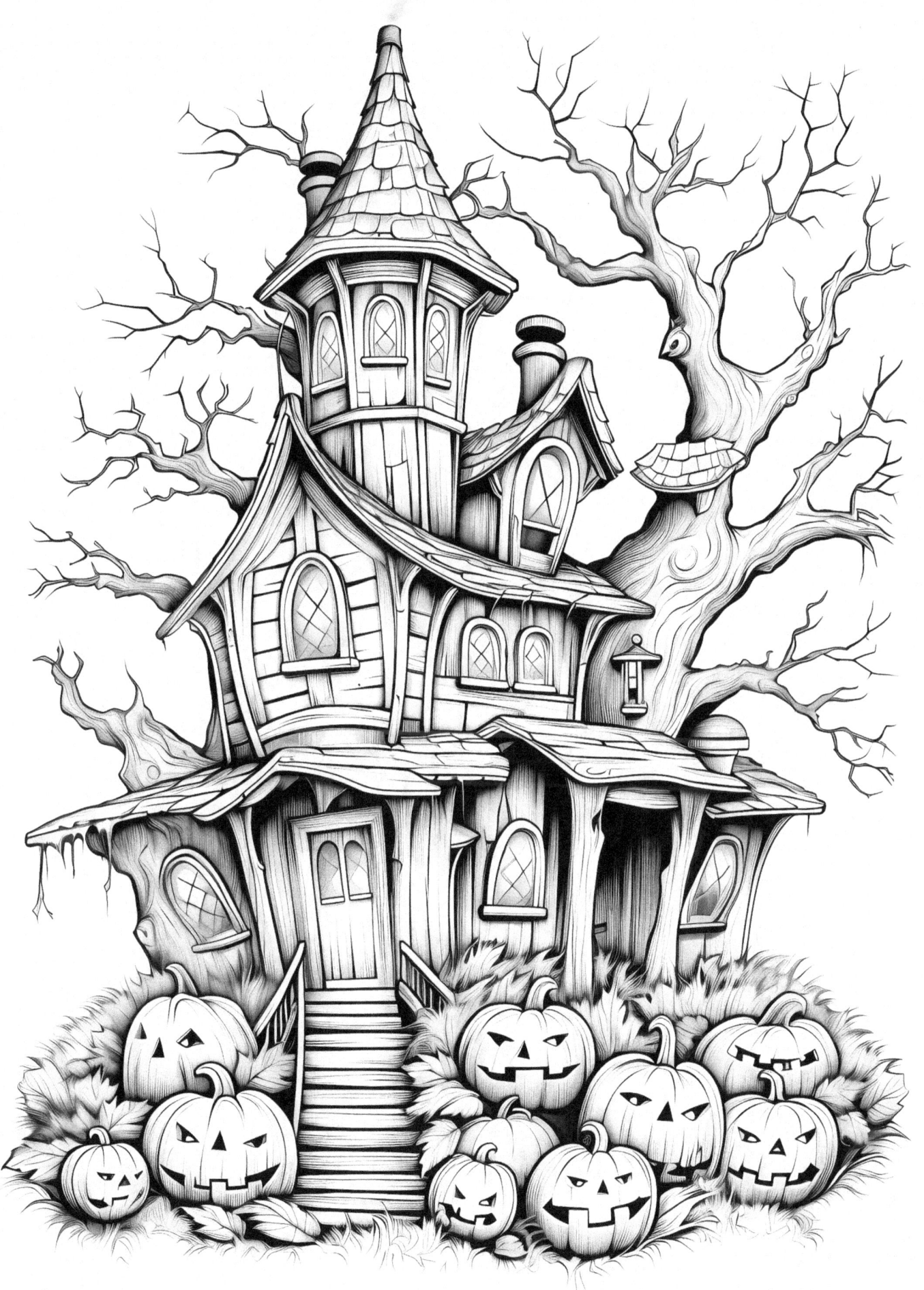

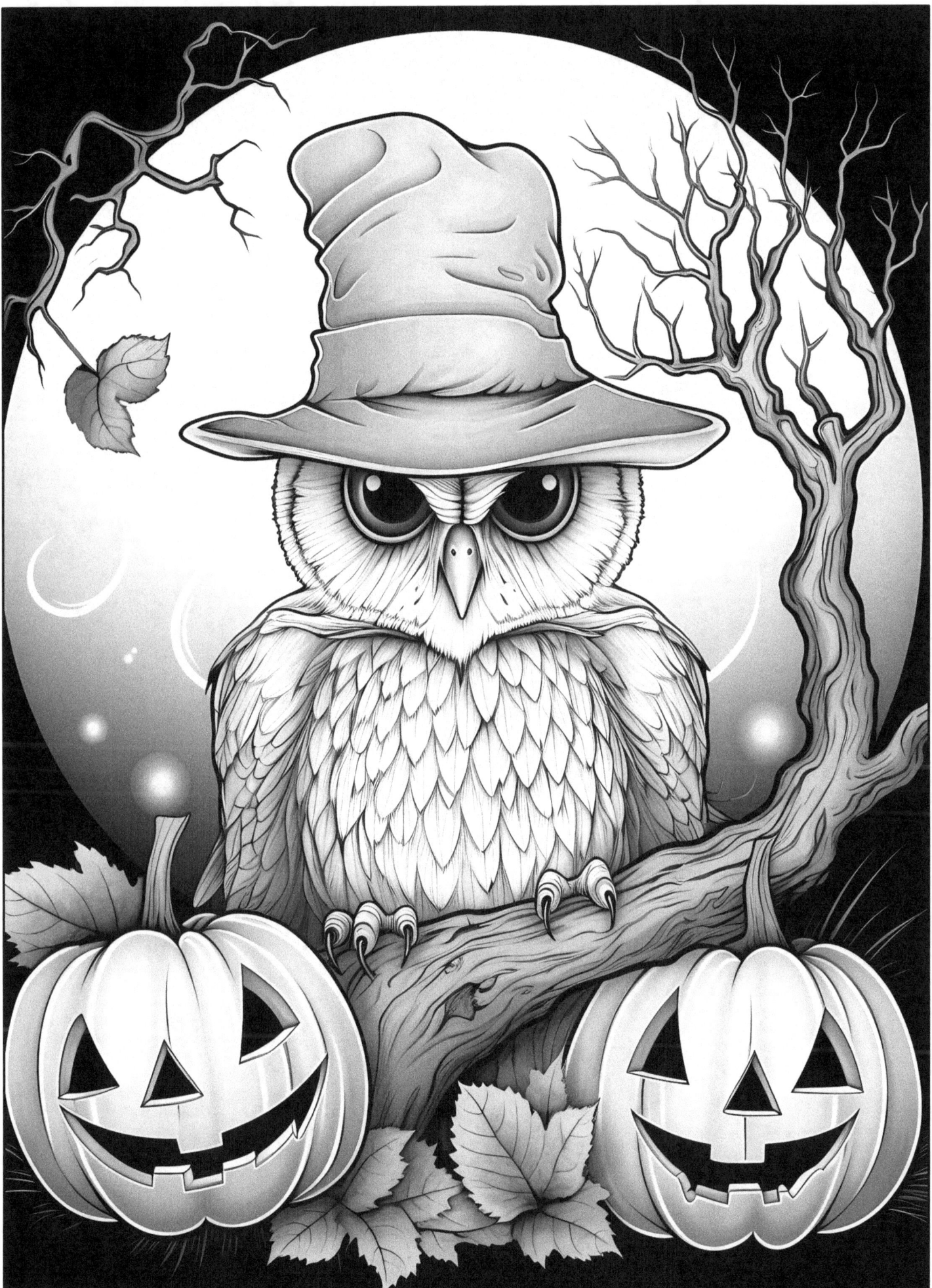

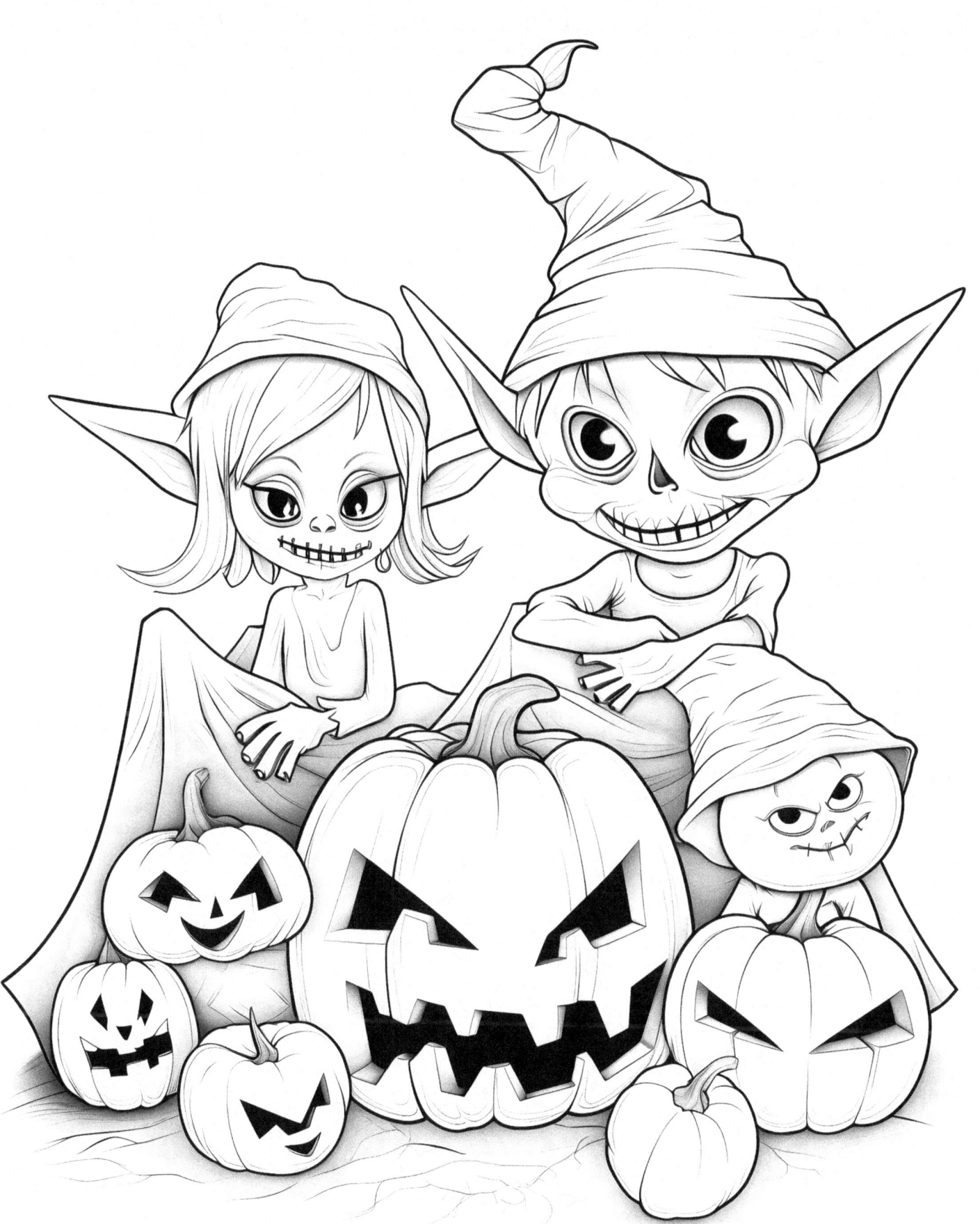

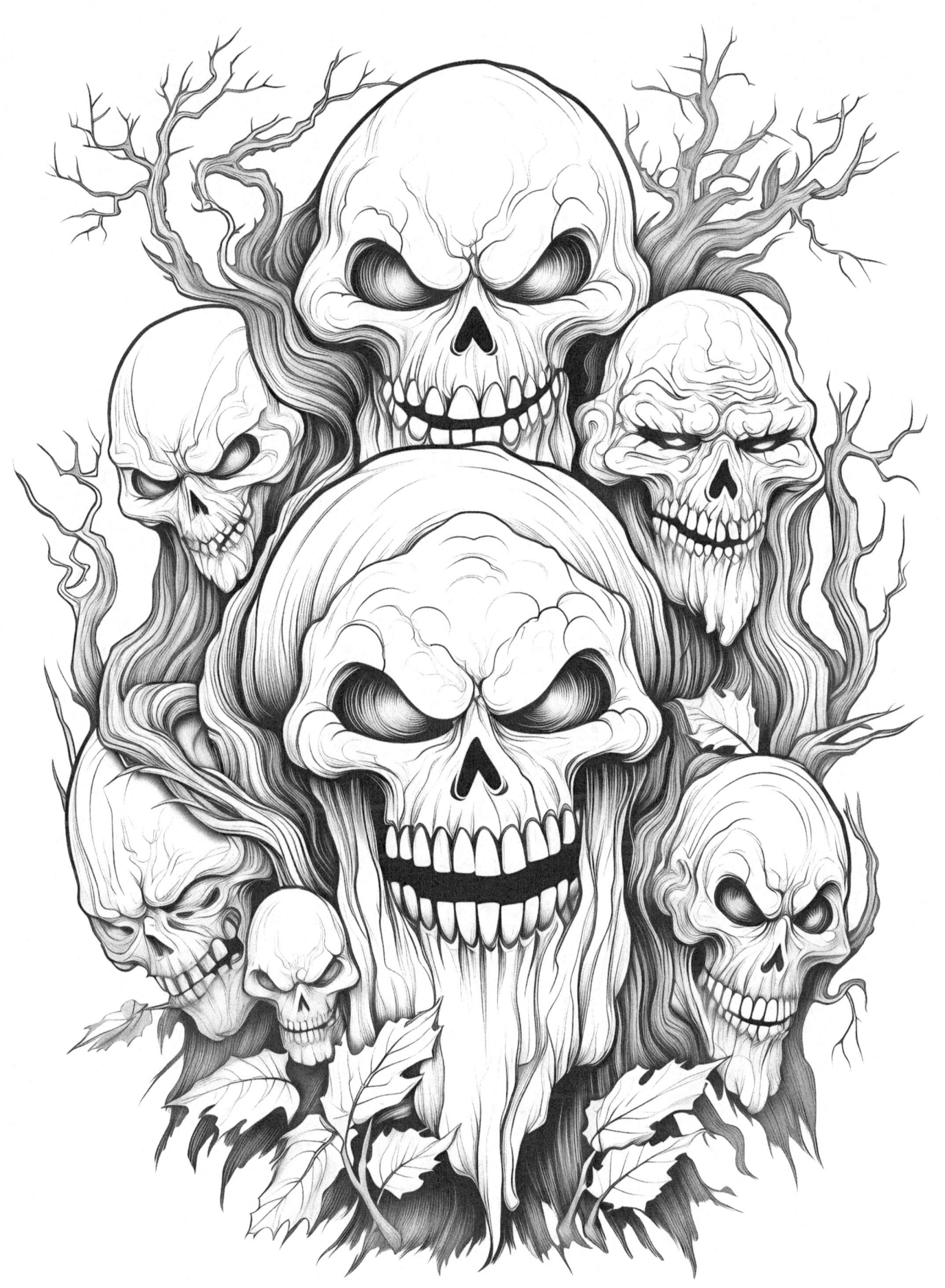